FOREWORD

The Bramshott and Liphook Preservation Society is
time to follow up his fascinating book on the Headl
the present work, which tells the long history of L
In it he has condensed for us the fruits of two years' t
interviews with the men and women who managed or served in the shops concerned
and repeated visits to borrow and copy treasured photographs, along with detailed study
of old Directories, newspaper cuttings and other documents. The result is a very special
contribution to the history of Liphook, written with the insight of someone who was
born and bred in the village. Liphook is lucky to have found such a chronicler.

The Society joins with Ian in thanking all those who have so readily helped him with
memories or pictures for this book. Correspondence about it should be addressed to
Ian Baker at 29 Headley Road, Liphook, GU30 7NS. A note inside the back cover
tells where this book, with our other publications, is on sale — and how you can get
it sent by post if required.

The book deals with fourteen shop-sites. Four of these are no longer occupied by
shops. In addition, a number of shops in Liphook stand empty at the moment. Yet,
if Liphook is to thrive and remain a delightful place in which to live, its individual
shops must thrive. The Society likes to think that Ian's book, as well as giving pleasure,
will remind readers of the importance of our shops to a healthy village life. We have
got our by-pass now — and extra parking space; the work on 'enhancement' of The
Square is about to begin. All this should make shopping in Liphook easier and more
attractive. Ian's book describes a village of individual shops run by local families, giving
'personal attention', of errand boys with bicycles or handcarts and bigger orders
delivered by horse and cart. Errand boys and the horses and carts disappeared long
ago. The remaining individual shops and the 'personal attention' — a very special part
of Liphook life — are likely to go the same way unless we all, old inhabitants and
newcomers, remember to shop at them regularly (and not just when we run out of
something at the weekend). Use 'em or lose 'em! Meanwhile, enjoy Ian's book.

October 1992   ADRIAN BIRD
                                      (Chairman, Preservation Society)

Note to 1997 Edition
**Liphook shops are still struggling because so many Liphook people shop elsewhere.
A note of major changes since 1992 will be found at the inside rear cover.**

CONTENTS

1

W. A. COYTE AND SONS, *8/10 London Road*

Coyte's in the London Road is the village's longest-running shop, trading here since 1913. However, business began on this site much earlier than that. Records show that in 1742 Samuel Woodbourne was renting out a shop, house and stables here, 'recently' built by him on a one acre plot cut out of Loampits Field; his tenant was Thomas Hack, a maltster, paying a rent of £8 per annum. In 1773 Samuel sold the property to Richard Denyer, a tailor. In 1810 his widow Elizabeth leased the shop to John Christmas; in 1833 the Denyers sold it to him, to finance the marriages of various Denyer girls. Trade directories list John Christmas here as grocer and farmer (also selling glass and china in some years) till around 1880. By 1881 the occupant was James Stent, draper and grocer, who employed three men and three boys.

By 1889 George Poole had taken over, calling the shop 'The General Supply Stores'. He lived in the shop house, with his wife Beatrice and daughter Mabel, and two members of his staff — one listed as grocer's assistant, the other as draper's assistant. The store advertised a very wide range of goods, including drapery, boots, clothing, new furniture, carpets, bedding, groceries, provisions, lamps, oil stoves, garden equipment, crockery, glassware, patent medicines and sporting cartridges. A second-hand furniture service was offered — buying, selling and hiring. In 1908 a special Spring discount of 1/- in every 11/- was offered. Typical prices of this time, in 1909, were china tea at 2/6d. per pound and potatoes at 2/6d. per bushel (8 gallons).

George advertised the business for sale in 1909, without success, and trade continued normally for a few more years. He finally sold up in 1913, and moved into the house next door (now No. 12 London Road).

In the meantime William Alfred Coyte had been born at Kingsbridge in Devon, where he became a draper's apprentice. He moved to London at the age of eighteen to learn more about his trade; there he met and married Constance Garrad, a draper's daughter. Soon afterwards they saw a notice for the sale of George Poole's business at Liphook and promptly bought it.

William took over the business in partnership with his wife's brother, Charles Garrad. They held a grand opening sale on February 8th 1913 and the following fifteen days. Tremendous bargains were offered, such as men's caps for 3½d., ladies' flannelette nightdresses for 1/6½d. and umbrellas for 1/11½d.

Charles Garrad was killed in the first world war, leaving William and Constance to continue and build up the business. A wide diversity of goods continued to be stocked, including most of the lines previously kept by George Poole. William was always ready to try new lines; he sold picture postcards of the area, and later even sold gramophone records at 6d. each.

Below the shop is a large cellar; this was used during the first world war as a restaurant. Does anyone know its name? For a while the cellar was used to grow mushrooms, for sale on the greengrocery counter, and remnants of the old gas lighting pipework can still be seen. The circular steel supports visible in the shop have their bases in the cellar.

The store was originally split into two departments, each with its own entrance, reached up stairs, and lit by gas lamps. The office and cash desk was situated between the two departments, and large skylights provided extra daylight above each section. The shop has its own living accommodation, with the entrance at the left front end of the building. It is named Devon House, for obvious reasons!

The rooms above the shop provide good storage, and at one time furniture was stored for customers. At the rear of the building were the stables, outbuildings, and coal yard, reached via a track from the Haslemere Road.

The left hand section, then and for many years, contained the haberdashery and clothing department. It was run by a staff of up to five, including Mrs. Coyte, and they wore navy blue or black clothing. Glass cases and drawer units contained much of the stock, with the larger goods carefully covered up each night by sheeting. Staff took customers' payments to the cashier, to return with the change and receipt.

Ivy Jackson joined the drapery staff in 1918, and worked here for a wonderfully loyal half century, during which time she married Stan Morgan (Stan's family ran a grocery business in Station Road). Ivy was a quiet, conscientious member of the staff, highly respected by her colleagues. They included Elsie Powell, Daphne Chandler, Mrs. Tilbury — and Ivy Trussler, who recalls joining on leaving school, at a wage of 5/- per week; she worked here until she joined the WAAF. Later, as Mrs. Ivy Howard, she served on the staff for several more years. Wyn Oliver (now Mrs. White) worked here from 1951 to 1963, some of the time as manageress. The department stocked clothing for local schools — such as Petersfield, Mill Chase and now Bohunt.

Coyte's also ran a draper's shop in Haslemere for some time, around the time of the second world war. Sometimes staff from Liphook were taken over by car to augment the Haslemere staff.

The name of Garrad did not entirely disappear when Charles was killed, for Miss Maude Garrad ran a drapery business in Station Road from the mid 1930s until 1948.

Coyte's right-hand section originally housed the ironmongery, hardware and household goods, and also the groceries until the early 1920s. The grocery staff wore white aprons, and included Charlie Payne and Mr. Chapman. Ruth Johnson worked in the shop for several years; she was well known for her involvement with the Liphook Amateur Dramatic Society, both on and off stage.

George Martin left school in 1936 and joined Coyte's for a couple of years, for a wage of 10/- per week, less 1/2d. deducted for insurance. He cycled to work from Hollywater each day to work in the shop, or delivering locally by bicycle, orders for the hardware, fruit and drapery. In two years George must have cycled many miles! He recalls that Coyte's ran a separate shop across the road in the single-story wooden buildings (now No. 3a, London Road); it sold greengroceries, cooked meat, cakes and chocolates, and was run for some of the time by Mr. Coyte's daughter Muriel (Mrs. Caesar).

Deliveries were made of coal, paraffin and household goods, at first by horse and cart. Harry Hooper was working on coal deliveries in the early 1920s, followed by Jack Davis and Walt Chiverton. Arty Funge joined the staff in 1925, and remembers helping Mr. Coyte with deliveries and receiving orders for drapery whilst on the rounds. Arty's first driving licence was bought for him by Mr. Coyte a couple of years later, and he had his first experience of lorry driving. Percy Read, a local haulier, and Mr. Coyte went to the Lennox Motor Company and purchased a second-hand one-ton Ford lorry, with left-hand drive. It had two forward gears plus reverse, and was started by a handle, and "was an unpredictable beast".

Arty worked on coal deliveries, some of the time with Walt Chiverton. They wore black shirts for this very dirty work. The coal was delivered by railway to the station yard, and a three-day limit was given to unload the wagon. If this was not met a demurrage charge was then levied. The coal was taken to their own yard ready for delivery. A typical price of the time was 'best kitchen nuts' at 38/- per ton. Arty left around 1933, and the coal deliveries continued for only a few more years.

Dick Frost followed Arty Funge, and drove vehicles for Coyte's for around twenty-four years, on either side of the war. His son David, who is a well known local postman, remembers helping his father in the school holidays. They were delivering paraffin and Calor gas, which was gaining in popularity. Other goods that David recalls were firewood, soap powders, washing 'blue' and Mazo washing tablets. George Osborn also drove for the Company, just after the war; Mr. Coyte taught him to drive.

William Coyte gave to the village much of his time and energies. In his younger days he was a member of local sports clubs, an interest which he never lost. He was elected to the Parish Council in 1942, serving for many years, including three spells as Chairman. He also served on the District Council. One of William's most important projects was the provision of the sporting facilities made available by a new recreation ground in the London Road. As an affectionate tribute to his many years and achievements in public service William was often termed 'The Mayor of Liphook'.

Other organisations that William involved himself with included the Liphook Horticultural Society, to which he belonged for over fifty years, the Parochial Church Council, and the Parish Club and Institute. He was a founder member of the Chamber of Trade in 1935. How ever did he find time to run his business so successfully?

William was a devoted family man, and his eldest son Hugh recalls how he, with his sister Muriel and brother Charles, used to love to play in the shop and rear yard. It was a magical place for young children, with lots of secret hiding places. The three of them would sometimes proudly help to deliver letters from the shop to local addresses.

Hugh went to work in the retail trade at Guildford and Bournemouth; in world war two he served in the Royal Engineers. During this war the flat roof of a rear outbuilding at Coyte's was used as a machine-gun post for the Home Guard. The shop was used to distribute petrol coupons, orange juice, baby milk, cod liver oil and the like and to sell National Savings Certificates. Nylon stockings appeared — but were at first very scarce and precious; a list of customers' sizes was kept.

Hugh joined his father at Coyte's in 1946, and took over the hardware department. His wife Betty also became involved in the business, in between raising their family of four daughters and a son. She ran the drapery department for several years; the third generation joined in when daughter Elizabeth commenced work in the drapery in the 1960s.

Hugh followed in his father's footsteps with his involvement in many local activities and organisations, particularly the Horticultural Society, the Chamber of Trade and the British Legion. Betty too has found time to play a part in village life, including active membership of the Womens' Institute and the Trefoil Guild.

William's younger son Charles served in the regular Army. He joined the firm in the early 1960s, working mainly on the administrative side, but also helping in the hardware section. So there were now three 'Mr. Coytes' for a few years! In the Coyte tradition Charles involved himself in village life, serving on the Parish and District Councils. He played a major role in the founding of our wonderful Community Care organisation, together with the formation of the Day Centre in the Midhurst Road.

Muriel was the eldest of William's family and worked at the shop for several years. In the 1930s she ran the greengrocery department: in later years, by now Mrs. Caesar, she worked in the office. Muriel will be best remembered for her work at the Public Library, particularly when it was situated at No. 5 London Road.

William Coyte himself continued work until 1965; in later life he lived in the Haslemere Road, with Hugh and family moving into Devon House. William's health declined and he died in 1968.

The business continued successfully through the 1960s, with the adjoining empty shop (No. 8 London Road) being bought, after the grocers there had closed. Part of the dividing wall was removed to create more room for household goods. With the yellow lines outside on the main road deterring parking, an entrance was formed from the Haslemere Road, allowing car drivers to park near the rear door of the shop. The old stable building was improved to serve as more storage.

Another of the third generation of the Coyte family, Hugh's son Simon, joined the company in 1973. Further improvements were made in the shop, particularly on the display shelving. Charles' health had deteriorated and he died in 1984, bravely carrying on his work and his village activities almost to the end. Muriel had also been battling with illness for many years, and died soon after Charles, whom she had been nursing so caringly. A special gateway, ramp and handrail at the entrance to Bramshott Church from Church Road perpetuates her memory and that of her husband John Caesar.

Hugh continued to work full time until 1986, when he officially retired. However he can often be found at the shop, particularly when an extra hand is needed in holiday times. Hugh was prominent in October 1987 after the great hurricane, when Coyte's were inundated with customers wishing to buy emergency equipment and supplies. Television pictures showed Hugh handling the queues of traffic in the Haslemere Road (we couldn't see the pictures in Liphook where we were without electricity for six days!). Hugh and Betty moved to a bungalow in the Avenue, and Simon and Mary moved into Devon House in 1980.

Deliveries have continued their importance in the post-war period, with Calor gas taking over from paraffin. The driving staff has included Mr. McGrath, Bob Fellows, Tony Elliott, Mick Osman and Chris Budd, who is married to Hugh's daughter Elizabeth. Trevor Bowley worked in the shop and on transport for around fifteen years; another of the shop's stalwarts was Miss Bennett.

A major reconstruction took place in 1988, when an open-plan shop was created for all the hardware and household stocks. The extension into the old grocers' shop became the haberdashery section. A new suspended ceiling was fixed, with concealed lighting, and new floor tiles laid. The shelving was laid out with self-selection made easy, but with helpful staff on hand. The office was moved to the rear outbuildings.

A staff of three full-time and three part-time are employed. David Sayer, the manager, joined in 1981, and Pam Bryder has valuable experience of working in other Liphook shops. Coyte's have always been proud of its traditional reputation as 'The Shop with the Stock', and is a bright, cheery establishment carrying on the old tradition in the modern trading style.

Simon has continued in the family tradition of joining in the village activities, and has been a member of the Fire Service since 1976. His grandfather would be proud to see Simon serving on the Parish Council, where he has recently taken over the responsibility for the Recreation Ground and Radford Park.

Coyte's continues to act as 'box office' for many local functions, and usually enters a float in the local Carnival. One can inspect planning applications here, or sign a petition against them should you wish to.

So thankfully Coyte's still continues to serve the village. In hard times people look back to bygone years, and locals still reminisce about the old times at Coyte's, when the shop was a little less orderly than today. The skylights would sometimes play up in heavy rain, needing a strategically placed bucket to catch the drips. The office was a place of mystery, and unseen stores of goods were kept in remote places. Often a customer would ask for some obscure item, more in hope than anticipation, only for Mr. Coyte to reappear triumphantly with the required goods!

Those days could not last, but are cherished memories to many of the older customers. They are perhaps summed up nicely by the pre-war Carnival programme:—

> To mention every thing that's sold
> At Coyte's we are not able,
> The few we do so we are told
> Do sound just like a fable.
> They have things to wear at which you may stare,
> Some things to chew, to starch and blue,
> And send smoke up the chimney flue,
> And some to shoot, to paint and glue,
> And for the house and garden too.
> Of glass and iron, and crocks and tins,
> Whatever you want, well just walk in!

E. H. MATTHEWS AND SONS, *Exchange House, Station Road*

Opposite the Railway Hotel in Station Approach, on a site now occupied by a large office building, stood one of Liphook's most revered shops, known to most people as 'Matthews'. Ask any of the slightly older generation which things they miss most in these modern times and 'Matthews' will be very high on the list. It was far more than just a grocer's corner shop. Facing Newtown Road and the Station Approach, it commanded great loyalty from both staff and customers alike.

A grocer's and baker's was founded here in the latter part of the 19th century and run by Walter Elliott until 1883. He was succeeded by Mr. and Mrs. Frederick Theobald Burbage, who moved over from Reading. Their staff lived nearby; Edwin Powell, a baker, and Edwin Stacey, a grocer's porter, both actually resided in the shop house. The name Exchange House was given to the building.

Frederick Burbage was a member of the first Parish Council in 1894, on which he served for over thirty years. He was associated with the formation of the local Parish Club and Institute in 1902 and was also Chairman of the Passfield Working Mens' Club. After his retirement in 1911, Fred continued to live in the area until his death in 1926 at the age of seventy-one.

For a few years, around 1907, a downstairs section was used by a firm of solicitors named Collier, Son and Sparkes. A piece of gauze with their name on it, which had been fitted across the window to be visible from the outside, survived to be shown at the local history exhibition staged by the Preservation Society at Bohunt School in 1980.

In 1911 Edward Henry Matthews moved to Liphook from Herefordshire and took over the business. He had previously been a tea traveller in Wales and the West Country, and tea blending became a speciality in his new business venture. Edward and his wife Annie Louise lived in the shop house, and they had a family of five sons and a daughter. In the years after the war two of his sons joined the business, with Wilfred working in the shop and Jack running the bakery and its rounds.

The business flourished. In addition to the groceries, provisions, confectionery and the bakery products, coal and coke were delivered around the area, from coal pens in the railway yard. These deliveries were made by horse and cart, and in time by motor lorry. The installation of the telephone, Liphook No. 107, was an asset for receiving orders. The water for the shop and house was obtained from a choice of two wells until the mains were connected up in 1926. Mineral waters and cartridges were also stocked.

The firm usually entered a 'float' in the Carnival, and the programme compilers did not leave them out of the poems, one of which read:—

In Matthews Store you're sure to find
Everything in the pastry line,
There's tarts and cakes and swiss roll light,
Which will be on view on Carnival Night.

Wilfred was married to Enid Trigg and they lived at Foley Lodge for a while, before moving into the shop house in the mid 1920s, when Edward moved to Edreston in the Avenue. Jack married Gertie Heath, a schoolteacher from Milland; they moved away in 1937 to run a small-holding in the New Forest.

Edward retired from the firm in the early part of the second world war, leaving Wilfred in sole charge. By now his family of Daphne, Geoffrey and Peter were growing up.

Life became very difficult during war-time rationing, with food supplies hard to obtain and distribute fairly. "It was a real headache trying to sort out all the various coupons". Bread supplies were reasonable during the war, but became difficult afterwards. All this posed great problems and Enid's health suffered badly; she died in 1951 aged only 51.

Meanwhile Wilfred's younger son, Peter, had attended Churcher's College at Petersfield, leaving in 1947 to work as an apprentice at Messrs. Kinghams in Farnham. After National Service Peter joined his father in the business in 1950, and the following year married Hazel Madgwick from Bramshott Chase. They lived in the shop house with father.

In 1948 a more modern bakehouse was built, by Johnsons the local builders from the Avenue, with triple-decker Collins gas ovens. A double shift was worked, with two men on days and two on nights. Besides the bread a selection of delicious cakes and pastries were made. A fleet of up to six delivery vans delivered around the district, including supplying some other shops at Rogate and Bordon.

The shop itself was extended on the ground floor, and a flat and office formed upstairs. Peter and his family then moved to Inglenook in the Avenue, next to Edreston. The coal business continued until the mid 1960's when it was sold to Comleys of Farnham.

Around this time things started to change in the grocery market, with the tendency towards self service and the large 'super store'. The big shops could buy and sell their goods much cheaper than in the smaller shops. However they could not offer the friendly and personal service of the smaller shops, and only stocked fast selling lines. 'Matthews' continued to please their many loyal customers for several more years. Unfortunately the bakehouse ovens started giving severe technical problems, and baking ceased in the early 1970s.

The final closure of the business took place on June 30th 1980, when the doors closed for the last time, leaving numerous happy memories for the staff and customers.

Arthur Dawes was a long serving staff member, joining in 1936 after working at Burgess's Stores, and stayed until the final closure. His happy memories include working with Fred Fuller, one of the chief bakers from the 1930s through the war when labour was scarce, until Fred's retirement past the age of seventy.

When Arthur delivered goods to the Redford area he would call at the house where his future wife Winnie was working, for a cup of tea and a chat. Inevitably the round became a little delayed, so Mr. Matthews tactfully suggested that Arthur made this his last call of the round.

Arthur Funge was employed from just before and during the second world war, running the coal activities, and still remembers driving the new Bedford lorry. Part of this time he was living at Rose Cottage in Newtown Road, for a rent of 10/0¼d. per week. He still doesn't know what the farthing was for!

Arthur, or Arty as we all love to call him, recalls the coal deliveries being tough, back-breaking work, mainly carried out in a team of two. Delivering one bag of coal to an easily accessible coal shed was not too bad, but carrying heavy sacks down awkward flights of steps was a skilled job. His assistant was Jimmy Jackson, who was deaf and dumb. This might at first seem to be a difficult situation, but Arty and Jimmy soon struck up a good relationship. A variety of hand signs were soon learned and understood by Jimmy. For instance, when about to deliver coal to Bramshott Church, Arty would hold his hands together as if in prayer, which Jimmy understood meant a trip to carry out the filling of the church cellar. This was a two-man job, with one person tipping the coal in and the other inside moving it into a tidy stack.

The heavy work played Arty's back up; he left for a slightly less strenuous job and was succeeded by Len Garnham, who had been bombed out of his London home. Len continued the good understanding with Jimmy Jackson, and they worked together for many years. When the coal deliveries ceased Len drove the bread and grocery vans. His youngest daughter June worked in the shop for a few years.

William Woods started work at Matthews around 1938 as an errand boy, delivering by bicycle, and then was taught to drive by Arthur Dawes. He spent many years driving the bread vans, which had sliding side doors, with shelves and a base for storage. William still remembers his days working with Arthur with affection, and he calls to see him often for a nostalgic chat.

Other van drivers included Ralph Goodyear, Bill Woodward, Fred Oliver and Arthur Bryant. Arthur had previously been a chauffeur at Waterside, and joined Matthews from 1959 until he sadly died in 1968.

Joan Eardley (née Phillips) commenced work at Matthews in 1943, and only left for a short while when her son was born. Joan recalls with affection her days working at the shop and making up orders, which would have been phoned in or placed by hand. Tea was still a speciality — a reminder of the early days. Some of her colleagues over the years were Alma Willis, Pat Coonan, Charlie Clinker, Grace Cannon, and Nancy West. Nancy often put up orders for delivery by her future husband Ralph Goodyear — they married in 1955.

Matthews had in 1935 been founder members of the Liphook Chamber of Trade, and the staff always enjoyed the annual window-dressing competition, which they often won.

When the day of closure arrived it did not pass without ceremony. Mrs. Maline Souttar, wife of the Rector, organised a farewell gathering of staff and customers. Each member of the staff was given a present and toasted with champagne. Mrs. Stanley gave a speech praising the years of loyal and friendly service given by the staff over the years. Five members of the staff had given a total of 185 years service — Arthur Dawes (44 years), Alma Willis (38 years), Joan Eardley (36 years), Len Garnham (35 years) and Willie Woods (32 years). Peter and Hazel Matthews had also been at the shop for 32 years, and thanked everyone for their loyalty and friendship.

So ended a century of service to the community, and before long this familiar building disappeared for ever, to be replaced by offices.

Peter and Hazel still live in Liphook, and have followed in Wilfred's tradition in their support of and hard work for the Parish Church. Peter has served for over twenty-five years on the Church Council, four years of which were as Churchwarden. His father Wilfred also served on the Church Council for around twenty-five years, so it's congratulations on their half century!

It is nice to report that some of the 'Matthews Spirit' still lives on in the village, with old work colleagues still keeping in touch. Miss Patricia Halahan, from Bramshott, was at the final day ceremony, and is one of many past customers who still talk of the good old days when one could phone up Matthews and have the order delivered the same day.

SMART'S THE BUTCHERS, *14 London Road.*

Albert Edward Smart, with his wife Harriet, moved to Liphook from Sussex in 1881 and started his butcher's business in a shop in the Square (No. 16). In 1894 he purchased for £210 a large four-bedroomed house in the London Road (No. 14) from Mary Jane Wood. Mary was the daughter of the previous owner Ebenezer Rowland who had died in 1891. The oldest deed shows the house as owned in 1870 by Joseph Scanner from Petersfield.

Albert formed a butcher's shop in the front right hand corner of the building:

it originally had a stable-type door. At the rear was a large garden, which bordered onto the boundary of the School (now the Library). In time a tennis court was built in the garden. At the rear were the stables, slaughterhouse, pens and pig-sties needed for such a business. Below the shop was a cellar which later became the cold room.

Albert and Harriet had two children, Olive and Albert George. In time Albert George joined his father in the business, and took over after returning from war service. During the war the shop window was shuttered up at night as protection against high-spirited passing soldiers. Olive worked at a nearby ladies' clothing shop.

The Smarts' meat was all English home-killed, except for some frozen lamb. One speciality was prime pickled tongues. Deliveries were made first by horse and cart, and then by Ford Model T van. The telephone was duly installed (Liphook No. 44), situated on the dining room wall and later in the hall.

Albert George and his wife Maggie had a family of three, Len, Jimmy and Jean. Len and Jean helped with the business, and Arthur Johnson still recalls helping Len to make sausages in the cellar. Jean helped in many ways, including keeping the books and driving the van, by now an Austin Seven. Jimmy did not join the business.

Len was tragically killed in the second world war, and Albert George sold up in 1953 to take a small-holding in Sussex. The new owners were Walter G. Johns, a high class butcher's from Haslemere, who also ran a shop in Fernhurst.

In 1969 a further change took place when Peter Baldwin of Messrs. W. F. Baldwin ran the shop, until 1977. Their main shop in Milford continues to trade in 1992. By now the buildings at the rear were not required by the butchers — they were used as stables for local horseriders.

The current owners, PRC Colour Processing, moved there from much smaller premises at 26, The Square in January 1979. The rear outbuildings have been converted into professional colour printing laboratories, which cater for customers all over the south of England. The shop remains very much in its original state and serves as the office. Rod Menzies is the managing director and his wife Liza is also a director, and they currently employ fourteen staff.

They are hoping to open a retail shop next door at No. 12A selling films and general photographic supplies, and also a passport service. Should this come about it will prove very useful in the village. When passing No. 14 it is worth stopping for a few moments to admire the solid brick building, with its various brick adornments, and realise that it is one of the few of Liphook's original butcher's shops still standing.

SILK AND CO., 5 *The Square*

Silk and Co. occupied No. 5 The Square, which is a good solid stone building, with partly rendered walls (since painted) and a steeply pitched roof. Records indicate that it was once part of the Anchor Hotel complex, serving as a 'tap', which usually means 'jug and bottle' or 'cheap bar'. It was also used to accommodate hotel staff and visitors' servants. The single storey building on the left was the stables for the business in horse and cart days.

Before Silk's, in the 1890s, Charles James and Company were already selling drapery, clothing, boots and furniture on this site. Water was obtained from a well between the house and stables. Below the shop was a good sized cellar.

By 1914 the business was taken over by George Silk and his uncle Alan. George had already worked for James & Co. as a lad and later full time on deliveries by horse and cart, so he already had an insight into the drapery world. The building came up for auction and was purchased by the Silk family for £1500. Alan ran the shop while George was serving in the 1914-18 war.

A thriving business served the village and surrounding area for many years, selling ladies', children's and gentlemen's clothing ("trousers altered at no cost"), bedding, towels, lino, carpets, shoes and haberdashery. Customers could try clothes on for size in the living room of the house. For do-it-yourself customers a supply of shoe soles, tacks and polishes were kept.

George lived at No. 54 Headley Road from 1918, with his wife Maude and family of Darenth, Patsy and Laurie, whilst Uncle Alan occupied the shop house. Both boys worked in the shop during school holidays, and Darenth recalls dusting the shoes and boots. Laurie commenced work full time in 1926 for a wage of 2/6d. per week, and by 1933 (when Alan died) he was dealing with deliveries whilst his father ran the shop.

A Ford T van was used for deliveries, with a regular round made up as follows:— Mondays to Grayshott, Churt and Frith End; Tuesdays to Passfield, Lindford and Bordon; Wednesdays to Milland; Thursdays to Headley, with Fridays used for any extra deliveries. Laurie would also lay carpets and linoleum if the customers so desired. The floor coverings were kept in a store at the rear of the premises.

The 1931 Carnival programme paid tribute to Silk's thus:—

> SILKS, satins, muslin rags,
> Boots, shoes, vanity bags,
> Cottons, woollens, laces, tweeds,
> Everything to suit your needs.

On Alan's death in 1933 George and Maude moved into the shop house, leaving Darenth and his wife Min at Headley Road. Although Darenth did not join the business, preferring the building trade, Laurie's sister Patsy joined in for several years. It was very much a family business, and Darenth's daughter Dorothy helped her uncle on the delivery rounds in the school holidays. She later spent nine years working at the shop, and sometimes joined Patsy on a trip to the London warehouses where stock selection was made. In 1935 George helped to form the Liphook Chamber of Trade.

Other members of Silk's staff included Ivy and Elsie Barnett, Wyn Berriman, Elizabeth Fellows, and for several years Stella Edwards, the dear wife of the well known 'broom-squire' and 'log man' Ted (whose reminiscences were included in *Liphook Remembers*, published by the Preservation Society in 1987). Laurie's younger daughter joined the shop from 1958, and Diane enjoyed the many duties, which included selecting stock.

George had already partly retired before he died in 1965, when Laurie and his wife Margaret moved to live at the shop. The business continued to serve the community until Laurie retired in 1976, thus ending almost a century of drapery retailing on this site.

However a new owner came along in Chris Hampshire, who had been running an electrical household appliance business at No. 1a London Road. As he was looking for a larger shop this was ideal, with plenty of storage facilities. Together with his late father John, Chris built the business up with hard work and good service to its present standard. The stable building was attractively converted into storage and living accommodation, and the well was made a feature inside the sitting room. In April 1985 he won one of the Preservation Society's first 'Enhancement Awards', for his remodelled shopfront, with its fine old-style hand-painted trade-sign in wood (not plastic!) The cellar has been made waterproof for extra storage, retaining the old beams in the ceiling.

Chris has been joined by his son Christian and they carry out the engineering work, leaving the shop in the capable hands of Pauline Green (who is the daughter of Roy Horlock). Chris is rightly proud of his achievements in refurbishing and improving the property in a very tasteful way. One disappointment was not being able to save the old wall panelling in an upstairs room which collapsed very suddenly one day.

Unloading large delivery vehicles has been a headache over the years, but has now become easier with the opening of the by-pass, which has removed the bulk of the A3 traffic. It's a far cry from the sleepy old scene of George Silk's horse and cart days.

FURLONGER'S and JEANROY'S, *20 Portsmouth Road*

William Furlonger started his butcher's business in Liphook at the end of the 19th century, in a small building adjacent to cottages opposite Osborne House in the Portsmouth Road (they were demolished later for widening of the A3 — the site is now a lay-by). He is believed to have taken over the business of Walter Wakeford.

After a few years he moved to a larger building further along, on the other side of the road (No. 20), and gradually built up his trade. The house is thought to have originated from the early 1800s, and featured some oak beams. It had been in the ownership of the Toop family (who owned a forge at Passfield) and trade directories of the middle 1800s record Miss Harriet Toop operating as a linen draper.

William had a small shop to begin with, but soon built a larger extension with a pitched roof. By the 1910s a good-sized shop had been created, with sliding sash windows; at the rear was a slaughterhouse. There was a paddock for livestock, and a nearby meadow was known for years as 'Furlonger's Field'. William also built the nearby pair of houses (No.s 16 and 18) and one was occupied for a while by the local police constable.

His family included three sons, Harry, Percy and Ernest. Sadly Ernest was killed in the first world war. Harry learned the butcher's trade and for a couple of years ran a shop in the Tap House in Liphook Square. Ernie Goodridge worked with him, before moving to Harris's in Station Road. Harry left the trade and went into agriculture, haulage and building, based in The Avenue. His partner was Mr. Gould, and together they built a row of houses in Headley Road (No.s 21 to 43).

Percy joined his father in the business, and played his part in its continuing success. They advertised as Family Butchers, poulterers, fishmongers and ice merchants, with 'families waited on daily'. The telephone was soon installed with the early number of Liphook 9.

Deliveries were made initially with horse and cart; a retired policeman, Albert Goodridge, used to help out. In time mechanical transport arrived to speed things out. Local signwriter Jack Chappell recalls doing the signwriting on their vans and trade bicycles. Once, after he had proudly painted the name on a van, old Mr. Furlonger looked at it for a while, then asked if he was going to do the hind quarters!

Don Fuller joined Furlonger's in the early 1930's, and worked both in the shop and in the slaughterhouse. Meat deliveries arrived from Smithfield, and fish from Grimsby, collected from Liphook station packed in ice. They also received deliveries of sheep, bullocks, calves, pigs, turkeys, geese, pheasants and rabbits. The pheasants were delivered from Stedham Hall, where sixteen gamekeepers were employed. Rabbits arrived from various sources and any which were surplus were sent to Smithfield on the returning empty meat lorries. Hides and skins were collected weekly by the Bermondsey Hide and Skin Company.

Among the staff at this time were Bert Wiltshire, Joe Smythe, Ralph Kirby, George Godfrey, Len Clarke, and Mrs. Kemp in the shop. Percy's wife Ellen rarely worked in the shop, but assisted with such things as crab dressing at a pinch. One of the main customers was the Sofio family of Bramshott Court, who employed many maids and gardeners. Don Fuller left in 1937 to work at the Co-op in Headley Road (now the Wavy Line Stores).

Charlie Stone worked at Furlonger's for a few years in the 1930s as errand boy and general help, carrying out such jobs as cleaning the windows, preparing poultry and game, and Christmas turkeys. Sausages were made by hand, and sage and thyme were grown in the shop garden.

Roy Horlock began in 1935 as Saturday errand boy for 2/6d. per day. He remembers riding to Hollycombe House and Forest Mere House on an afternoon trip. Sometimes the Anchor Hotel would telephone through a late poultry order, which might well mean a frantic dash to Miss Larkworthy's poultry farm at Passfield to get supplies, and then back to the shop to prepare the birds for delivery. Roy commenced full time work in 1937, left for a short while, and then returned until RAF service in 1941. His work included everything except cutting the meat; by 1940 he was allowed to drive the van. Another of Roy's errands was a trip to Liphook Square to buy buns from Burgess Stores and an ounce of St. Julian tobacco from Shipp's (No. 22 The Square), for Mr. Furlonger senior.

Live bullocks were delivered for slaughter by Percy Read's lorries and kept in a paddock for a while. Roy Horlock recalls that in 1940 one Aberdeen Angus bullock was particularly lively. It charged through two brick walls and on up the main road towards the village, sending everyone diving for cover. Roy and a colleague Stan Grant were returning from their lunch break and came face to face with the bullock, which they managed to turn into the rear of the Anchor Hotel after it narrowly missed a funeral procession. The animal then proceeded to charge through a succession of fences and hedges until it ended up in a paddock at Westlands Farm a long way down the Longmoor Road. The farm's owner, Major Robert Kennedy, was not amused! The bullock became calmer for a while and was escorted back towards The Square, where it once again broke loose. The local population had again to 'take emergency evasive action' into the nearest shop. The bullock turned into the rear of the Anchor Hotel, but this time it swung left instead of right, and found itself in Furlonger's own meadow, and Roy and Stan heaved an exhausted sigh of relief. The damage to the brick boundary wall was repaired by the Royal Engineers manning the nearby searchlight battery; they placed a memorial plaque in the wall, which survived until 1992. One slight consolation when meat rationing began was that no more live bullocks were delivered for slaughter!

Roy's brother Tony also worked at Furlonger's for a while, until 1944, and Roy himself returned after war service for a further spell until leaving to work for the bus company.

The cashier's work here was very hectic and skilful, with the butchers calling out weights of meat, which had to be converted into the price to be paid, and a ticket/receipt written out. Freda White was cashier for several years until the early 1930s, and was succeeded by Minnie Hillman. It was here that she met her future husband Don Fuller; she continued at the shop for many happy years.

Other members of the staff after the war included Percy's elder daughter Joan, Alf Barr, Jack Blank, Miss Miles and Mrs. Furlonger's niece Audrey Garnham. Alf Barr stayed right until closure, and now works part-time at The Meat Market in Midhurst Road. The slaughterhouse was no longer used; it now housed the sausage making machine.

By 1963 the business had been taken over by Paul Jeanroy and his wife Peggy, but the name of P. Furlonger was retained. Paul originated from France and was partly trained in Switzerland. His continental experience and charming manner kept a good class of business going, including regular orders from local hotels and restaurants. He was featured on the BBC TV series 'Bon Appétit'.

The shop regularly won the Chamber of Trade window dressing competition. Depsite the rather difficult parking, the business continued into the 1980s when Paul Jeanroy retired to Petersfield and later to France. A company from Liss, G.W. Read & Son, took over the business for a few years, but trade lessened for some reason; perhaps the busy main road put people off. Closure came in 1988, just a few years before the by-pass which might have allowed the business to succeed again. This was not to be as the shop and ground were purchased by a property company, which proceeded to smash down the building and surround the site with lethal barbed wire, lying derelict for several years and presenting an eyesore to passers-by. Fortunately no young child was injured on the way to the Church Centre. The sad sight of this familiar part of the Village's heritage being demolished left many people asking why no protection is given to such historical buildings. Perhaps we should remember Furlonger's with a light hearted extract from the 1931 Carnival programme:

> To show yourself a glutton
> For the very nicest mutton,
> Or a great desire for veal reveal,
> Should your heart not find relief,
> Till you get the finest beef,
> Why, then with us it is you ought to deal.
> Should you have a frantic wish,
> For the better type of fish,
> Or fall a victim to the craze for game,
> Should it become a habit,
> To eat, each meal, a rabbit,
> FURLONGERS supplies are all the same.

FAULKS AND BLANCHARD, *38 Newtown Road*

In 1914 a fishmonger's business was started by Mr. Faulks and Mr. Alex Blanchard, situated in a lean-to building at the side of Quarry Bank (No. 38) in Newtown Road where it joins the Midhurst Road. The fish was delivered from Grimsby daily and collected from the railway station at 6 a.m. and then prepared ready for delivery. The fish was packed in ice boxes. Daily deliveries of ice were received from Messrs. Colebrook of Godalming in summertime, and at less frequent intervals at other times. The little room was almost filled by a huge ice-box and by a copper where they boiled winkles – and "delicious lobster tails from South Africa". After a while poultry, pies and sausages were also supplied.

Local deliveries were made by trade bicycle, and a van dealt with the longer trips. The staff included Don Fuller, Ron Reynolds, and Alex's son Jack. Tony Oliver's first job in 1935 was there, and he remembers manning one of the two trade bicycles, delivering round Liphook. Every Monday the bicycles were given a thorough check-over ready for the week's work.

In 1941 Mr Blanchard had a strange encounter when a stag "bounded from Chapel Common as he was driving along the Langley Road and charged his van. Its antlers pierced the side of the van, missing Mr. Blanchard by inches. The stag wrenched itself free and made off." His partner, Mr. Faulks, died during the war; in 1945 Vic Dent joined the business. Mr. Blanchard retired in 1949 and trading ceased. His son Jack then worked for H. Oliver's, the builders at Bramshott and later ran his own plumbing and heating business from his house in Church Road.

Arty Funge (on r.) & Jimmy Jackson, outside the Railway Hotel, about 1945, on their coal delivery round (see p.10)

Mr. Smart the butcher (see p.11) about 1918. Note the shutters! – kept in box behind him when not in use.

George Silk at the door of his shop (now Hampshire's electrical shop) about 1940 (see p.13).

21

James's, the first shop at 5 The Square, about 1900 (see p.13): site now Hampshire's electrical shop.

William Furlonger & family, early 1900's, before the shop was enlarged (see p.15).   The three boys are (l. to r.) Percy, Ernest, Harry.

23

Closing day at Matthews' 1980 (p.11). L. to r.: Miss Halahan, Mrs. P. Beard, Joan Eardley, Wm. Woods, Alma Willis, Arthur Dawes, Mr. & Mrs. Matthews (Colin M. behind), Len Garnham, Pat Coonan, Mrs. Lane, Mrs. Souttar, Mrs. Stanley.

Lena and Fred Hiscock with daughter Nowell, 1930's (see p.34).

25

Fairbairn's Stores, early 1900's; they preceded Bromley's (see p.31). In 1992 a video shop.

George Harris, butcher, with his daughter Dorothy (Mrs. Moreton), late 1920's (see p.36). Cellar railings on l.

27

William Oliver's shop, 19 Station Road, decorated for King George VI's Coronation Day 1937 (see p.39).

Burgess's Stores (Alldays site), about 1916 (see p. 41). George Smith on r.
Lloyds took over the Bank on l. about 1920 and moved to Ship House 1963.

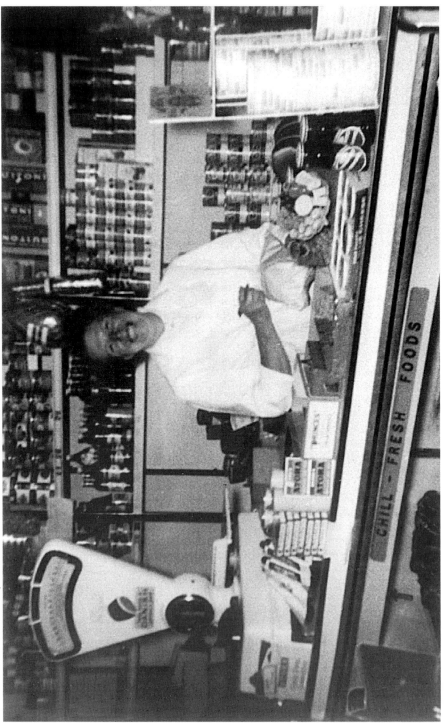

June Elliott at Burgess's in 1960's (see p. 43)

E.H. BROMLEY, 'THE PEOPLE'S STORES', *No. 6 The Square*

'The People's Stores' was situated in one of Liphook's oldest buildings, parts of which date back to the 1500's. Recent building renovations have exposed very old roof timbers and some daub and wattle plastering. In 1992 the rendering was removed from the front elevation to reveal two differing types of stonework. It looks as if the right-hand section of the main frontage was built at a later date than the left. The current shop-front may well have been installed at that time. Access from the living accommodation into the shop was down some steps, through a thick wall; this wall was probably the original front wall of the property, which would have been end-on to the road. The extreme right-hand addition was built much more recently.

Early records list Mrs. Mary Hobbs (née Denyer) as the occupant in the 1840s and 1850s; she ran a sub-post office here. In the Crimean War (1853-56) she would post up the war news for public viewing after first reading it herself.

In 1859 Ebenezer Rowland, a stationer and coal merchant, lived here. In 1867 Alfred Fewtrell was in residence, before founding his grocery shop on the corner of the Midhurst and Haslemere Roads (see chapter on Burgess's Stores).

By 1881 Eliza Scammel, a sixty year old widow, was running a stationer's business here; ten years later Emily Shepherd was operationg a newsagent's and fancy goods shop.

By 1895 John Grey Fairbairn had opened up the shop as 'The People's Stores', selling a wide range of merchandise, including china, stationery, glass, toys, fancy goods, confectionery, brushes, hardware, cigars and tobacco and patent medicines. The medicines may well have ceased around 1903, when a chemist, E. Gane Inge of Haslemere, opened a branch almost next door, at No. 12 The Square (currently Hampton's). Among the china sold by Fairbairn's were special cups and saucers depicting a view of The Square. John played a part in village life, and was elected to the Parish Council in 1907. He took an interest in the formation of the Parish Club and Institute, and in 1901 presented it with a hundred candle-power lamp, together with two guineas for their funds.

By 1911 The People's Stores had been taken over by Edgar Holdsworth Bromley, who moved to the area from London. He married Miss Hogsflesh, a local lady; while he was serving in the 1914-18 war his wife and mother ran the stores. The business continued in much the same way as under Fairbairn, and before long the telephone was installed (Liphook No. 24). They published picture postcards of the area for a few years.

At some time the name 'People's Stores' was dropped, and the simple name of E.H. Bromley only was used. They didn't employ many staff, but people

F. C. HISCOCK, 54 Midhurst Road

Situated in a line of three shops in Midhurst Road opposite the entrance to the Ordnance Depot is No. 54, an early 1900s brick-built shop and house. Trade records show occupation by Mr. Henry Couchman, a seed and corn merchant, from around the first world war until 1929.

Arthur Dawes recalls working there in his spare time as a schoolboy, making deliveries with an old barrow cart. These trips were made before school on weekdays, and all day on Saturdays. A local trip to Dr. Allen's in The Square would earn him 4d., to Goldenfields 9d., a big load of horsefeed to Frimstone at Griggs Green would earn 1/6d.

Fred Hiscock took over the business in 1929, with his wife Lena Anne. He had previously worked at Bordean House near Petersfield as a gardener, and the shop was his first business venture. They sold corn, seeds, seed potatoes, flour, tea — and animal feeds, including 'Tottenham Pudding' for pigs ("pig-swill and other bits and pieces"). Their dried peas were purchased mainly by small boys for their pea-shooters!

Deliveries were made locally, at first by motor-cycle and side-car, and then by a T type Ford. Fred proudly drove off in his new car, but didn't know how to stop it, so he had to keep driving around until the petrol ran out. In 1944 a yellow Austin Ten van was purchased from Kingshott's dairy in Station Road (No. 5).

Fred and Lena were joined in the business by their daughter Nowell, which was very useful while Fred was on Home Guard duties. In 1947 Nowell married Edward Brandrick, who was a crane driver at the Army Depot opposite, where he completed 43 years service. He helped with the shop deliveries at weekends. They had two children, John and Joy.

Fred retired in 1963, and he and Lena both died in the mid 1960s. However their grandson John Brandrick had started to help in the school holidays, and joined the business fully in 1971.

Hiscock's did not always rush to avail themselves of modern services. They had well water until 1942; they were only connected to electricity in 1951 and the telephone was not installed until the early 1970s. Most orders were placed with calling salesmen, but sometimes a trip had to be made to the nearest telephone box to place an urgent order.

As business increased an extension was built onto the existing shop, with access to the garden and store buildings at the rear of the premises. Some of the older part of the shop still retains its original matchboarding on the walls and ceiling.

A good variety of pet and animal foods are kept in stock, obtained from up to thirty different suppliers. Customers can buy as much or as little as they

34

wish, measured and weighed from larger sacks or containers. None of those infuriating tough polythene pre-packed goods here! A selection of seeds and fertilisers are stocked, but not seed potatoes, which are difficult to store. At one time pets were available, including rabbits, budgies, parrots, hamsters, mina birds and goldfish.

A visit to Hiscock's is very refreshing, with some of the old world charm of less frantic times. The shop window is full of interesting adverts for animal-related items. John and his staff offer a friendly and helpful service, with nothing too much trouble, and sensible prices. They will still deliver goods if required. If John is not around he may well be out with the local fire brigade, which he joined in 1974.

J. SMYTHE, *1 Newtown Road*

Joseph and Susan Smythe opened a small shop in 1926 in the building on the corner of Newtown Road and Station Road. It is a traditional brick building, but has an interesting feature with its wall facing the road cut at an angle. Previous occupants had included Metson the Jeweller in the years before the first world war, and Mr. Jackson, who was a watchmaker, also selling sweets and tobaccos.

The Smythes opened up mainly selling drapery, and also continued the confectionery, which was supplied by Luff's of Haslemere. They enlarged the window to give better display of the goods. Joseph himself would travel around the area, trading in an assortment of goods, whilst Susan ran the shop, and also handled a domestic agency.

The shop continued until rationing started and then reverted to a home until 1966. Then one of their sons, Patrick, with his wife Dolly opened up a dry cleaners. The clothing was collected and cleaned by The Regis Laundry from Bognor Regis. It was always a great pleasure to call at the shop to be given a warm welcome by Dolly, with her lovely, happy disposition. Pat and Dolly continued the business until 1976, when they moved away from the shop.

The Liphook Valet Service then took over the premises, moving there from their old shop at No. 13 Headley Road. Their headquarters are at Petersfield, with Liphook one of many branches. The shop is looked after by Sheila Lambert, who has worked there since 1984. The rooms above are currently a solicitor's offices, and the house section is occupied separately.

G. HARRIS, *Butcher, 6 Station Road*

George Harris was born in 1879 at Burford in Gloucestershire, and first worked on the railway. After a few years he went to work for Messrs. Corner's the Butchers in London, who had a contract to deliver meat to the tented army camps at Bordon and Longmoor. George was involved in the meat deliveries and eventually came down to Liphook to look after things on the spot. Delivery to the camps was of course by horse and waggon.

At the age of 21 George had married Maude Lilley; they set up house in Hackney. When they moved to Liphook they first stayed at the Passfield Oak Inn. As the family increased further moves were made, to Newtown Road, Liphook, and to a larger house in Portsmouth Road named Sundale Villa. George then had a large family home built in Station Road, with plans to start his own butcher's business, and the family moved there in 1912.

The war interrupted George's plans, and he served in Ireland as a regimental butcher. During the war, part of the house was used as a barber's, by George Gabler (senior).

After the war George and Maude were at last able to fulfil their ambitions, and when the necessary permit was obtained the shop opened. At the front of the shop a cellar was constructed, covered with a concrete roof, which supported the front garden. Its access was via a flight of steps, protected by iron railings and an ornamental iron gate. The cellar was always cool and ideal for the storage of meat. When electricity arrived a refrigerator was placed in the shop, and the cellar used to house the sausage machine. During the second world war it made an ideal air raid shelter.

A large proportion of their meat was obtained from Messrs. Borthwicks, but pigs were killed at the rear of the premises.

George Harris is remembered as a very generous man, who would help poor families with an extra helping from time to time. The week after Christmas each customer was given a joint of meat, and a lovely calendar. George and Maude had nine children and several of them worked in the shop at various times. Dorothy and Kathleen both worked at the cash desk, and George (junior) and John also spent time with the business.

Water was obtained from a well in the kitchen, pumped up to a storage tank in the roof. Lighting was initially by gas lamps; the shop was one of the first to be on the telephone (No. 17 Liphook) which was very useful for receiving orders. The delivery service was very important, with local trips being made by bicycle and longer journeys by van. Ernie Goodridge was a stalwart member of the staff for almost all of the shop's lifetime, and combined driving duties with the cutting and preparation of the meats.

Ernie Smithers recalls starting work in 1937 when leaving school, at a wage of 2/6d. per week. In addition to making deliveries on the trade bicycle, his work included scrubbing down the butcher's block at the end of each day. Ernie was encouraged to learn to drive by Mr. Harris, which stood him in good stead for his later career as a lorry driver.

George served in the local Home Guard during the second world war and carried the business on for a few more years whilst rationing was in force, which he found very trying, unable to please all of his many customers. His health by now was not good, and he retired at the end of rationing, and the shop closed. His youngest daughter Phyllis, who was a Queen's Milliner, returned to Liphook to care for her parents, and continued to live at No. 6 after they both died — George in 1958 and Maude in 1965.

With the assistance of Charles Dunkley, who was an antique and carpet dealer from Liss, Phyllis reopened the shop as Liphook Antiques for around ten years.

The final chapter began in 1986 when George's grandson Michael Harris and his wife Susan reopened the shop as a very nicely presented delicatessen named Poppet's Pantry. Despite its very friendly service and good stocks it was just that bit too far from the main shopping precinct, and closed in 1988. It might have been more successful if the 1992 car park had been built ten years earlier! (Sue Harris is now the senior librarian at Liphook Library).

Phyllis then decided to move to a smaller property and hoped that the house would once again be a happy family home, and perhaps a shop again. However this was not to be, as the agents sold it to a property company, and they were only interested in the ground, together with the house next door. It was a very sad sight to see this lovely brick building being demolished to make way for blocks of flats — which are named Harris Court, after the family. One of the workmen there even said to George's daughter (Mrs. Moreton) that it made him sad to be carrying out this contract. Phyllis was able to salvage one memento of the happy past in the form of the ornamental iron gate, with the letters GH wrought in the ironwork.

LIPHOOK,
TELEPHONE :
2239.

M..194

Bot.
of P. FURLONGER,

Family Butcher, Fishmonger and Poulterer.

37

A. MORGAN and W. OLIVER, *19 Station Road*

A handsome brick-built row of three shops, with living accommodation above, is situated in Station Road, by the stretch of higher pavement and the pillar-box. They are numbered 19 to 23. The first two were built in 1902 by local builder Abraham Harris, followed by No. 19 four years later. A close inspection of the front wall between No.s 19 and 21 will reveal a join in the brickwork, and until recently No. 19 had no attic dormer window. It did however have a small single-storey front extension to the left of the main shop.

The first occupants of No. 19 in 1906 were Messrs. G. Crawley and Son, who sold groceries, provisions, 'colonial' meat, and were agents for Lipton's Tea. Coal was delivered from a yard at the rear of the building.

The shop was taken over in 1912 by Arthur Morgan. He moved there from Ashford, where he previously ran a grocer's shop and had learned his trade through a five-year apprenticeship. He decided not to continue the meat business, as he knew little about it and George Harris was soon to open a butcher's shop opposite. The butcher's hooks were removed from the front extension, and a stock of hardware and earthenware set up. The coal deliveries were also discontinued, but deliveries of groceries were made daily in an old Ford Type T van. They also delivered paraffin from a tank in the back of the van. Bicycle deliveries were carried out by the 'Saturday boys'; one of these was young Eric Jackson, who had to take great care when delivering boxes of eggs. Orders could be placed by the telephone — Liphook No. 60.

Arthur and his wife Ada had a family of seven, and the youngest, Don, was only four when his mother died in 1920. Ada's sister Miss Letchford also lived at the shop and cycled daily to Headley to teach at the local school on the green. Together with Ada's eldest daughter she helped to bring up the younger members of the family. Don still remembers with affection the Saturday evenings when the family would gather for one of her delicious cooked meals.

Arthur was joined in the business by two of his sons, Stan and Arthur junior. For a few years the shop was also a sub-post office, which saved a fairly long walk to the main post office, then in London Road. Arthur (junior) left to work for Burgess's Grocery Stores, first at Godalming and in due course at their Liphook branch. Stan stayed with his father until the shop closed in 1936, and later worked at the Army Depot in Midhurst Road. He was married to Ivy Jackson, who worked for many years at Coyte's, and whose parents spent some time running the The Deer's Hut public house (approximately 1907-27).

Meanwhile at Burgess's Stores William Oliver had been a master baker for many years, and was also running a turf accountant's business in a small way. As clients were calling into the shop to place bets this created a very sensitive situation, so he decided to start his own business. He traded for around seven years from a room at No. 27 Station Road, selling groceries, bread and cakes, and also building up his bookmaker's business to over a hundred clients. Grocery deliveries were made on a trade bicycle with a carrier front and back. He was assisted in collecting the bets by Mr. Baxendale and Mr. H. Farmer. Mr. Farmer lived in one of the two old cottages which then stood on the site of the present lay-by in the Portsmouth Road, opposite Osborne House.

When Morgan's closed in 1936 William Oliver took over the grocery business, also selling bread and cakes (the bread came from Buck's Bakery in Grayshott). The hardware department was replaced by the turf accountancy. The good-sized accommodation suited William and his wife Laura as several of their large family were still living at home, gradually getting married over the next few years. One of his sons, Peter, started work for his father on leaving school, making deliveries by bicycle, and in due course in a 'baby' Austin van.

Peter married Rhona Moss, and they lived for a while in Headley Road, returning to live at the shop around 1950 (Peter had been away on war service and returned in 1945). Another son, Tony, joined the business in 1945. He was in the shop when a very smartly-dressed man came in and asked to see '*the* Mr. Oliver'. ''I fetched my father (more or less retired by this time), who was feeding the pig! The visitor said, 'Your window display of Crosse and Blackwell products caught my eye. I want to congratulate you, Mr. Oliver — it is fantastic! Would you do me a favour and come and have a drink with me at the Links Hotel? I am Crosse of Crosse & Blackwell!' '' Tony's father died in 1952 after some seven years in retirement.

Tony left the business in 1960 to work in insurance, where he became well-known and popular with his many customers. Peter and Rhona were now running the business, although Peter's sister Eve had assisted when her mother was alive. Another sister, Winifred, had married Sid Smith and they ran the Railway Hotel, where film shows were given in an upstairs cinema room. Peter was the regular film projectionist, and many well known films were featured.

The front extension had become rather below par and was demolished in 1964, with the turf accountancy housed in a lean-to building to the left of the main shop. Sadly Rhona died in 1971; her younger daughter Anna gave assistance with the groceries until this part of the business ceased in 1976.

Peter continued the turf accountancy until his death in 1982, when Tony returned to assist his own son Robin to run the business. This continued until 1988, when Tony Love took over and a modern shop front was installed. The front extension was rebuilt in 1989 as a separate shop unit.

Peter's elder daughter, Barbara Pitt, still works in Station Road, at The General Wine Company, both in the shop and on the delivery rounds. It is nice to report that she is following the family tradition of friendly and efficient service.

THE GALLEON TEA ROOMS and PARTNERS STORES,
4 London Road

At the start of the century Liphook was endowed with its first Main Post Office in London Road (No. 4), on the present site of the Midland Bank, just beyond the Green Dragon Inn. Until then postal services had been available in a local grocery store. As the population increased a larger Post Office was built in Portsmouth Road, opening in 1933. When the population increased even further the Post Office closed in 1989 and returned to the grocery store! However that's another story.

With the old post office redundant in 1933, it was put to a variety of uses, including the sale of second-hand furniture by Mrs. Wide, who also started a shop in Headley Road (now the Job Centre).

Soon after the war ended the building became the Galleon Tea Rooms, opened by Mr. and Mrs. Merrick. At the front a picture window was formed, with pretty curtains. Inside, around fifteen tables were situated, with additional tables on the rear lawn in summer — all with waitress service. Business commenced at 9 a.m. seven days a week, with the serving of morning coffee, biscuits and home-made cakes. From midday three course lunches were available from a varied menu, and later on afternoon teas, scones and cream were the temptation, available until 6 p.m.

A mixture of regular customers, passing motorists, cyclists and walkers were catered for. Several local ladies were frequent visitors and had their own 'personal' tables, including the eccentric Mrs. Hill from No. 127 Haslemere Road, who always commandeered a favourite corner table. To please passers-by a delicious ice-cream selection was available from a special serving hatch in the front wall.

Among the staff dealing with the cooking and serving were Dorothy Kemp, Jean Dillingham, Jean Sawkins, Priscilla Burt, Anne Bramley and her daughter Olive who helped at weekends.

The Tea Rooms closed in 1954 and Partner's Stores, a grocery business, was opened here by a partnership of five shop directors from Haslemere. They already ran a shop in Haslemere High Street, from where Ernest and Elsie Kimber moved over to Liphook, leaving their son-in-law Ron Boxall in charge at Haslemere. Ernest had originally moved to the area from London in 1943.

The name Galleon House was retained, and initially a few coffee tables were provided to satisfy thirsty callers who hadn't heard about the change. Partners Stores retailed high class groceries, greengroceries and provisions, including home-cooked ham. They also specialised in coffee beans and teas, including 'Cancho' tea. One of Ernie's daughters, Janet, helped with the book-keeping, and a reliable delivery service was provided by Doris Miles and Ivy Read.

Other members of the staff included Alan Cooper, Mary Gauntlett, Audrey Garnham, Cilla Collins and Jean Pritchard.

In his spare time Ernie was a keen golfer, and his son Ray became a professional golfer. Gardening was another of Ernie's hobbies.

The shop closed in 1963, when Ernie's health wasn't so good, and the building was taken over by the Midland Bank, who moved there from No. 20 The Square (which is in 1992 the right-hand end of Border Insurance).

BURGESS'S STORES, *2 Haslemere Road*

A grocery shop and bakery, with living accommodation, was built on the corner of Midhurst Road and Queen Street (Haslemere Road) in the later 1800s. It was built on the site of some old cottages by Alfred Fewtrell, who had previously traded at No. 6 The Square. He was joined in the business by his son, also named Alfred. Until the new main post office in London Road opened at the turn of the century the Fewtrells ran a sub-post office in their shop. Alfred senior's daughters Caroline and Arabella were post office assistants.

Alfred junior ran the business for five years after his father died in 1895, after which it was sold to Charles Burgess of Godalming. Alfred turned to agriculture for his occupation, and for many years operated from Lowsley Farm in the Avenue.

Charles Burgess, in addition to his Godalming store, ran other shops in the area, including Haslemere, Shottermill, Lion Green, Hindhead and Farncombe. Early views of Liphook show that the shop itself was situated in the right-hand front section of the building, with one main window facing Queen Street and a similar one facing the Midhurst Road. The entrance was angled between the two windows, and consisted of a pair of doors, reached up some steps. The doorway to the living accommodation was in the front centre, and a pair of large doors on the left served some covered accommodation or storage.

By 1907 the left-hand section had been converted into a bank, run by the Capital and Counties Bank Ltd. By the 1920s Lloyds Bank had taken it over. The shop itself was fairly narrow at the front, running to a wider area at the back. The cash desk was situated inside the door on the left, and was in touch with the various counters by means of an overhead wire and cup system.

A long polished hardwood counter ran from front to back, with shelves behind stacked with groceries, and beers, spirits and Gilbey's wines. Tempting baskets of table fruit were placed on the counter, and anyone feeling a bit leg-weary could sit on a handily placed chair. Rows of drawers were filled with

41

sugars, dried fruits, spices and other delicacies. These were dispensed in bags expertly made from blue paper (probably manufactured at the Paper Mill at Passfield — now Passfield Industrial Estate).

At the further end of the shop the provisions were displayed with lots of boxes and tins full of goodies to choose from. Most were not pre-packed but were weighed out in exactly the quantities required by the shopper. Biscuits could be chosen from various tins, and any broken ones were served to schoolboys at knock-down prices.

A coffee grinding machine was situated in the window facing the Midhurst Road, and below the shop was a large cellar. Burgess's were early subscribers to the telephone — Liphook No. 11.

The name 'Queen Street Grocery and Bakery Store' was painted on a wall panel above the pair of entrance doors. The bakery was situated at the rear of the premises, and access to the mixing bay was up some wooden steps. The ovens were modern, with coke firing, and the bakery floor was smartly tiled. A dough making machine was tried but was not successful.

At Easter hot cross buns were baked, and local people would wait patiently for one 'straight from the oven'. Christmas and wedding cakes were made to order. The bakery staff started work at 4 a.m. and included William Silk, William Oliver, J. Beagley and Arthur Dawes.

A staff outing in a motor charabanc was arranged annually, with a stop made at each Burgess's store to pick up more passengers. Everyone was given 2/6d. to spend, and meals were booked at a seaside restaurant.

Mr. Burgess appointed a manager to run the Liphook Store, and for many years this position was filled by Mr. W. Wright. Mr. Burgess made a weekly visit to the store, in a chauffeur-driven Rolls-Royce. Mr. Wright drove an Austin Seven car. The delivery vehicles were far more basic. Arthur Dawes's first job on joining the store was as Fred Oliver's van boy; the old Morris van had wooden spokes and no front brakes. It was kept in a building opposite the shop; this was once the stable where the two delivery horses were stabled. Arthur also worked in the Bakery before leaving in 1934 to work at E. H. Matthews, who ran a similar business. Fred Oliver gave loyal service for many years, from before the first world war until after the second world war.

George Smith was the backbone of the shop for very many years, from the early 1900s through to the early 1960s. He started as an errand boy on leaving school, and became a prominent member of the staff. He acted as manager in holiday times at various other stores within the company as well as at Liphook. George was absent for a couple of years when he joined the Surrey Constabulary, and also during service in the first world war.

Many members of the staff were trained by George, including Harold Baker, starting from 1927. Harold still remembers George as a friendly fair man who would stand no nonsense and was a good teacher of the trade. One of his sayings sticks in Harold's memory still — "One boy — one boy; two boys — half a boy; three boys — no boys". When the Bridge Farm Dairy horse-drawn milk cart reached Burgess's Shop the horse 'Jimmy' would pull up smartly to wait for a bun to be brought out from the shop. George would always enjoy this little diversion from the day's work.

The carnival programme paid its 'poetical' tribute as follows:-

> You get the 'Wright' goods here, my friends,
> For Beagley to the pastry tends,
> You leave your orders there with Smith,
> Oliver delivers them forthwith.

Arthur Morgan commenced work at Burgess's after working at his father's grocery shop in Station Road. He married the manager's daughter, Winnie Wright, and himself became the manager in 1931, when Mr. Wright retired. He and Winnie moved into the shop flat from their home in Queen Street (Haslemere Road). They had two daughters, Sheila and Betty — Sheila worked in the shop office during and after the war. Arthur was manager until the late 1940s when he left to run his own cake shop in Shottermill for a few years.

The shop front was painted in green with gold leaf lining. Jack Chappell, the decorator and signwriter from Headley Road, recalls the occasion when he was putting the finishing touches to the paintwork near the shop doorway. Lady Keppel from Bramshott Lodge (whose husband, Sir Derek Keppel, had been Governor of the Royal Household) put her hand on the wet paint: as she was wearing white laced gloves some hasty cleaning had to be carried out with turpentine! Jack also did all the signwriting on the delivery vans.

June Elliott joined Burgess's shortly after the second world war, and worked here for twenty-five years, mainly on the provisions counter. She would arrive at work by 7.45 a.m. to prepare for opening time at 8.30, removing the skins from large cheeses and cutting them to size. The prices ranged from 1/6d. to 2/- per pound. Hams and bacon were also prepared, and gammon rashers had to be cooked at the shop. June was taught by George Smith, who always stressed the need to avoid leaving lots of small pieces. The shop closed at 5.30 p.m. and, by the time the tidying up had been done, it was 6 o'clock or after.

When June started at Burgess's Arthur Morgan was the manager, and later Ron Morgan, who was no relation. Other work colleagues June remembers were Miss Gauntlett, Neville Flarry, Pam Swan, Sheila Morgan, Joan Roberts and Ethel Oliver, with Fred Money and Fred Oliver on the deliveries.

Pam Swan worked on the cash desk from 1956 to 1964, and in 1961 first met her future husband George Bryder, who was working on building alterations to the shop. A new shop front was installed, with a more central doorway, and the floor was lowered. However the personal attention continued, and the van deliveries went on for a few more years. Pam recalls serving paraffin at 2/4d. per gallon, while it could be delivered for a penny more!

Customers could then have weekly or monthly accounts. Major customers included the Anchor Hotel, and officers' messes at Chiltley Manor and Bramshott Camp.

In 1963 Lloyds Bank moved out, to go to its present home, and the shop was further extended to make use of the extra room. Florrie Pritchard worked at the shop in the early 1960s, and recalls visits made to inspect the shop by Mr. Avens the shop inspector.

Joy Brewer was employed from 1966 to 1973, and in 1968 was married to David Lush who was a clerk at the nearby Lloyds Bank. Joy recalls working with Tony Horlock, Michael Weeks, June Elliott, and Winnie Dawes in the office. By now the bread was being delivered from Smith and Vosper, with the bakery out of use.

From around this time the shop had a succession of owners — Lipton's, Moore's and Presto. In 1988 it was reopened by Circle K, after a refurbishment programme, opening for long hours, and popularly termed a 'convenience store'. In 1989 Kevin Hart took over the franchise: he has moved into the flat to live with his wife Sharon and family. He employs up to thirty-five full and part time staff, who are needed to cover the long opening hours, seven days a week. The customers enjoy meeting many of the local staff members, including Sue Young. Sue has worked in several shops in the village, having spent several years at Coytes and earlier at the Liphook Valet Service in Headley Road. Cilla Windle is supervisor, and enjoys working back in the village of her birth. When she was Miss Collins she worked at Partners Stores in the London Road. As June Elliott is her aunt, there is a family connection here again.

Kevin has taken a keen interest in local history, especially of his shop, and his office walls are adorned with old pictures of the shop and the village. He has joined the local Chamber of Trade and is pleased to be creating a more friendly, village-type atmosphere within the confines of modern trading methods. He would dearly love to modify the external livery of the shop, should funds permit.

By some strange irony Liphook's post office is now back where it was a century ago — it's a funny old world!

44

PEACOCK'S STORES, *24 The Square and then 8 London Road*

In the early 1920s Coyte's stopped selling groceries, and one of their employees, Mr. A. Peacock, decided he would start his own grocery business, in a small shop in Liphook Square (now No. 24).

The premises had previously been occupied, since the 1880s, by John Kelsey and his wife Annie, running a boot and shoe repairing business. John was regarded as a true artist at his work and could make even the worst shoes as good as new. The needs of the poor were as painstakingly met as those of the better-off. Local children loved him and playfully teased him. Sadly, John was a cripple but could move swiftly with the aid of his crutch. Being a Methodist lay preacher he would quote words by Charles Wesley — "lame as I am, I take the prey". John died in 1913 and his wife continued the business for a few more years.

Mr. Peacock then opened his new shop, with the assistance of his wife. He was rather short in build, while she was very tall. Some of her remarks could truly be said to have gone over his head! He also kept pigs in a field off the Headley Road, tended by local lads, including young Tommy Vale.

Jim West started work at Peacock's in 1924, at a wage of 15/- per week, working in the shop and making deliveries by bicycle. Two of his colleagues were Fred Barker, who lodged with Mr. and Mrs. Hall in Station Road, and Charlie Clinker. Charlie's father worked in the village at Wakeford's the saddlers, just around the corner (No. 18 The Square).

The accounts were kept in an upstairs room by a pretty young lady living opposite the shop at Tweenways (Nos. 15 and 17) named Connie Caesar, who later married a local young carpenter and joiner named Ted Baker (the author's dear parents).

In 1929 the business was purchased by Mr. George Standfield, who lived at Billericay in London Road. He had previously run a grocery business in Grayshott, before moving to Bramshott in 1922. He built his own house, and carried out vegetable farming, supplying various shops in the locality, and did not actually work at Peacock's. He appointed Charlie Clinker as his manager, at a wage of £2/10/0 per week, plus a small annual bonus.

Another member of the staff was Jimmy Atherall, a cheerful young man whose father ran a smallholding in Tower Road. Jimmy later left to become a Prudential Agent in Liphook for twenty-six years, and will be remembered for his dance band which played at many local functions. He sadly died at the early age of 57 in 1968, but his son-in-law Mr. Knapp is following in his footsteps in the same insurance work in Liphook.

Jim West continued with the deliveries, by now with a BSA four-wheeled drive vehicle purchased from Moss's Garage in the Portsmouth Road (currently the Jet station). Jim was a welcome caller with the customers as he always knew the latest snippets of local news. An additional help to the shop was the installation of the telephone — Liphook No. 89.

Peacock's usually entered a float in the Liphook Carnival, with their 1934 entry being entitled 'Red, White and Blue'. In return the carnival programme entered a ditty in their praise:-

> At Peacock's the manager's name is Clinker,
> Whose statements we thought very bold,
> "With prices we never do tinker,
> Our groceries are the best that are sold".

Meanwhile, further up the road at Sunnyside (No. 8 London Road) beyond the original old post office, in the early 1900s a Miss Alice Halsey had started a ladies' outfitters and fancy drapery — and as agent for Dr. Jaeger's Sanitary Woollen Clothing! This shop was taken over by 1911 by Miss Mary Ann Wakefield, who also sold baby linen, hosiery, greetings cards, notepaper, and Fuller's confectionery and cakes! The shop was reached by some steps and had small windows on either side of the doorway. Schoolgirls loved to call on their way home from the school (now the Library) to buy some sweets, a delicacy, or an item of stationery. Miss Wakefield's assistant was Olive 'Queenie' Smart, a sister of Albert Smart the butcher, living nearby (at No. 14).

For a few years in the 1930s the shop became The Bon Marché, and was run by Mr. and Mrs. William Coleman, telephone Liphook No. 137. The Colemans' relationship was not always harmonious and often after an evening spent with his friends at a local tavern George would have to sleep in a suitable hayloft! At night in the dark, during the war, he would use the white line in the middle of the Headley Road as a guide to take him to The Square. This was fine till he met somebody doing the same, but going in the opposite direction, with a collision often the outcome!

Around 1936 The Bon Marché closed and Mr. Standfield moved his Peacock's Stores here, as more room was available. Messrs. Croad's of Portsmouth installed a larger shopfront, and the outside shop walls were covered with glazed tiles. The old shop on the corner was then rebuilt by Mr. Williamson, son-in-law of the Kelseys, as a hairdressing establishment — which it still is, several owners later (currently named 'Orchids').

Charlie Clinker continued as manager in the new shop; his Wednesday half-day was often spent playing cricket for the Liphook Wednesday eleven. Jim West remained on the staff until 1940; another popular staff member was Millie Woods, who was a member of the well known Phillips family. Her husband Sid did Mr. Standfield's gardening; they lived at Jubilee Terrace in Headley Road for many years.

Other workers at the shop included Neville Flarry, Fred Benham, Nina Cross, Doris Miles, Joy Stillwell, Kath Hughes, Kathy Homewood and Anne Bleach. Anne used to drive the van, until she left to drive her father's lorries at J. J. Bleach Contractors.

During the rationing period Charlie Clinker was kept busy sorting out all the coupons, which often was a task carried out on the dining room table at night at his home in Tower Close, with the valued assistance of his family. In later years his young son Dennis used to like going out on the delivery van in his school holidays.

Below the shop was a cellar, reached via a trap door in the floor, which was useful for the storage of goods needing to be kept cool. One day a water-pipe burst, resulting in a flooded cellar. Fortunately a new consignment of soaps had not yet been placed in the cellar for storage, or there might have been the cleanest cellar in the country, or soapsuds bubbling up through the trap door.

In 1947 the shop was taken over by Messrs. Pink's, a group from Portsmouth; they continued to trade here until the mid 1960s. Charlie Clinker left in 1957 and went to work at E. H. Matthews in Station Road till he died in 1960, sadly well before retirement age.

The last manager at the shop was Alan Gard, who now runs the Passfield Post Office and Stores in a very friendly and helpful manner. Other staff members in the final years were Marie Brewer and Connie Berry. After closure the shop was purchased by Coyte's and an opening knocked through to extend their shop; in 1992 this section is used for the haberdashery counter.

THE LIPHOOK CHAMBER OF TRADE

A meeting was convened in the Liphook Village Hall on Tuesday 29th 1935, and the first committee of The Liphook Chamber of Trade was formed. The officers were:-

President — Mr. K. G. Poland (from Downlands at Bramshott)
Secretary — Mr. W. A. Coyte
Chairman — Mr. J. J. Williamson
Treasurer — Mr. A. Morgan

"The auditors to be Mr. Felton and the current Midland Bank Clerk."
The committee was formed by:-

Mr. W. H. Stoneman (from Haslemere)   Mr. W. Matthews
Mrs. Rea (from Bramshott Stores)   Mr. W. Coleman
Mr. G. Silk   Mr. A. Blanchard
Mr. E. Bromley   Mr. S. Bailey (fruiterer)

A meeting was held a month later and 22 members handed in their names. In addition to the above, there were present:-

Mrs. D. E. Wide	Mr. P. Furlonger
Mr. F. Hayward (draper)	Mrs. A. Gollop (grocer)
Mr. F. Payne (watchmaker)	Mr. Adams
Peacocks Stores	Mr. Griggs
Mrs. L. Hillyer (confectioner)	Messrs. Smorthwaites (chemists)

The large majority of members were shopkeepers, many remembered in this book. J. J. Williamson ran a hairdresser's and newsagent's in the Square (now No. 7), and was elected to represent the Chamber on the National Body.

The first subscription was 10/6d.; this was reduced to 7/6d. a year later. Meetings continued at regular intervals, held at the Church Rooms, Devon House (Mr. Coyte's residence) or The Green Dragon. None were held between 1942 and 1948.

In 1935 a meeting objected to the proposal for a Liphook by-pass on the grounds that:-

1) it would affect business interests and building development;
2) the necessity did not exist and the expense was unnecessary;
3) the alternative of road widening should be seriously considered.

It is easy to be wise over fifty years later, but they could not possibly have predicted the huge expansion in the traffic on the main road, and the arrival of the yellow lines. No doubt they had serious concerns about losing the passing trade of the time. It was appropriate that members of the present Chamber were the prime movers and organisers of the 1992 By-pass Opening Celebrations.

Naturally the Chamber of Trade has always taken a keen interest in local affairs, particularly in recent years car parking facilities and litter problems. Special efforts are made to brighten up the village at Christmas with seasonal lighting, and a carol service in The Square.

The Chamber have collected and provided over £7000 for the formation of the Liphook Medical Aid Fund to provide much needed medical equipment for the benefit of local residents using the Surgeries.

In 1985 a Dinner was held to celebrate the half century of the Chamber's formation; the annual window-dressing competition still takes place. The current membership numbers around forty, most of whom are shopkeepers.

The Liphook Chamber of Trade will be adding their experience and enthusiasm to the opportunities given by the removal of the heavy through-traffic and the forthcoming improvements to The Square.

Major changes since this book was first published (1992)

P2.   Coytes' historic shop closed 30.9.94. Occupants since 1995 are IML ('Interactive Meetings Ltd.'), multi-media computer experts providing 'audience response services', etc. IML have uncovered a fine painted glass shop-sign installed by Pinks over one of the doors (for Pinks see p.40, para. 4).

P.7(foot)   Soon after Coytes closed, David Sayer on 5.11.94 opened Liphook Hardware in Station Road, next to Barclays Bank; Pam Bryder assists him.

P.21(foot) The site was at last developed in 1993, as Nos. 1-12 Churchfield Court, with houses on the Portsmouth Road frontage and on the drive at the S. side.

P.29(foot) 'Film Rack' closed about 1993; the site is now occupied by Inwood Stoves – who also sell a striking range of bric-à-brac.

P.44(foot) In October 1994 Circle K was replaced by Alldays, a friendly 'convenience store' like Circle K but with more attractive windows. The Post Office facilities remain.

This book and our other publications can be obtained from 12 London Road, Liphook, Hampshire GU30 7AN (mornings only) and from Sesame Health Shop (The Square), Blackwell Press (Newtown Road) and the Coffee Shop (Station Road). Orders by post should be sent to 12 London Road; prices in brackets below include postage.

Liphook Shops Remembered £2.50   (£3)
Liphook Souvenir £2.50 (£3)
Chiltley Place and Goldenfields £3   (£3.40)
Conford from Domesday to Victoria £2.50   (£3)
Liphook Lives £2   (£2.40)
Liphook Calendar (dated Liphook 'news' from 1066 to 1989) £2   (£2.40)
Liphook and the Headley Road £2   (£2.40)
Liphook Remembers £2   (£2.40)
Liphook, Bramshott and the Canadians £2.50   (£3 – by air to Canada £3.70)
Walks around Liphook £1.50   (£1.90)
And, published by the River Wey Trust,
The Southern Wey: a Guide (maps and colour plates) £2.50   (£3)

Matthews' Stores, Station Road, probably 1920's (see pages 8 - 11).
Site now occupied by Stackhouse Poland Insurance Brokers (Exchange House).

ISBN 0 9511829 4 3

ISEKHUA EVBOROKHAI

YOUR HEART & MIND

PRICELESS POSSESSIONS WORTH PROTECTING

Your HEART & MIND

PRICELESS POSSESSIONS WORTH
PROTECTING

Isekhua Evborokhai

Your Heart & Mind: Priceless Possessions Worth Protecting
Copyright: © 2019 Isekhua Evborokhai
Phone: +353861690217
Email: remisek@yahoo.com
ISBN: 978-1-911312-08-6

Published by: Lacepoint Publishing
www.lacepoint.ie I Email: services@lacepoint.ie

Printed in the Republic of Ireland.

Dedication

To my family; nuclear and extended!

Acknowledgement

All thanks to God Almighty for once again finding me a worthy vessel and granting me Your grace and divine inspiration to bring this message to Your world.

To Remi, Judith, Nathan, Nicole and Jessica; you remain a very special part in the fulfilment of my dreams. Thank you.

To my spiritual parents: Thanks for your prayers, support and positive influence.

To my parents Godfrey and Hannah Evborokhai and my siblings; thank you for your prayers and for believing in me.

To the family at RCCG Ireland, for letting me serve Christ's body, thank you.

Contents

"Guard your heart above all else, for it determines the course of your life." Proverbs 4:23 (NLT)

Introduction

EVERYTHING WE DO IN LIFE KICKS off from our hearts and minds. Our actions, inactions and reactions. Our body language, our responses and silences – all of them are channels that output the thoughts of our hearts and minds.

The heart and mind; though different are very closely related. As a matter of fact, they are both mentioned very many times throughout the Bible; and many times, in the same sentences too! They are used interchangeably many times as we will see; but yet different. In the course of reading this book, you will find the terms also used interchangeably too; simply because of the very important linkage they both share.

The initial focus of this book was based solely on the revelation I received about how our minds influence our lives and how we could change our lives by changing the way we thought; but the more I searched the scriptures and researched the subject matter, the more I discovered how entwined the mind is with the heart. And although used interchangeably in this book, I concluded that for completeness the heart and mind are "best served together".

There are several definitions and connections of the heart and mind, but let's first consider how the

Almighty God connected them both when He quizzed Job in Job 38:36

*"Who gives **intuition to the heart** and **instinct to the mind**? (NLT)*

The Amplified Version says:

*"Who has put **wisdom in the innermost being** [of man, or in the layers of clouds] Or given **understanding to the mind** [of man, or to the heavenly display]?" Emphasis mine*

From this verse of scripture and the different translations we can decipher that the heart referred to here is not only the physical heart; the muscular organ that pumps blood to the lungs and keeps us alive. But something much more!

The heart is the part of our being, responsible for controlling our desires, emotions, hopes, beliefs, judgement, decisions and aspirations. The Bible refers to it as the *"holder"* of intuition; the ability to understand something without the need for conscious reasoning, and the *"holder"* of wisdom. It is the seat of emotions and teller of truth. That is why for instance, when we lie to cover the truth, our hearts tend to beat faster.

A polygraph test is used to determine the truth from a person by monitoring breathing rate, pulse, blood pressure, etc. - all outputs from the heart.

The mind, on the other hand, is responsible for controlling our intellect, reason, and thoughts. It is the seat of consciousness, the will, the intellect, the seat of opinion. It includes our perception, and memory. The Bible refers to it as the *"holder"* of instinct; a natural ability, the *"holder"* of knowledge. It is also the part of a person that thinks, reasons, and remembers. The mind is a very powerful "tool" God blessed everyone with.

This brings me to the first connection between the heart and the mind. Most, if not every innovation ever recorded in history started off as a thought; *a product of the mind!* And the driver of such innovation is the dream of success; *a product of the heart!*

Let me submit another interesting connection between the heart and the mind:
The way we think is based on the contents and inclinations of our hearts!

Between the heart and mind, we find the very core of all human existence! Because together, they determine the course of our lives! They determine whether we succeed or fail in life; they affect all our life's choices and ultimately determine if we live or die! Without a doubt, both combined form a formidable powerhouse! That is why the Bible admonishes us in Proverbs 4:23 to:

"Guard (our) hearts above all else, for it determines the course of our lives." (NLT) Rephrased

The KJV of this verse of scripture admonishes us to *"Keep our heart with all diligence . . ." Emphasis mine*

The New Century Version says:
"Be careful what you think, because your thoughts run your life." Emphasis mine

The Common English Bible says:
"More than anything you guard, protect your mind, for life flows from it." Emphasis mine

To guard one's heart or mind *with all diligence* involves employing all you can to protect it; it requires a deliberate and conscious effort. It is to meticulously watch over it to protect it from damage, harm, or pollution. And also, even more importantly, to control it; keeping it in constant check.

When we continue to read from verse 24 to 27 of Proverbs chapter 4 (AMP), we see the first five steps we need to take to run our lives successfully.

Verse 24 - Abstain from lies and trickery
"Put away from you a deceitful (lying, misleading) mouth, and put devious lips far from you."

Verse 25a - Be careful what you look at; stay focused on what is good, right and true
"Let your eyes look directly ahead [toward the path of moral courage]."

Verse 25b - Be a person of integrity and avoid distractions
"And let your gaze be fixed straight in front of you [toward the path of integrity]."

Verse 26 - Be circumspect
"Consider well and watch carefully the path of your feet, and all your ways will be steadfast and sure."

Verse 27 - Don't entertain any forms of compromises
"Do not turn away to the right nor to the left [where evil may lurk]; turn your foot from [the path of] evil."

We are aware of the effort governments, organizations and individuals put into protecting items of value like art treasures in museums.

They use laser detectors, alarms, patrol guards, etc. to protect these artefacts against theft and vandalism.

They employ curators who come in to polish these artefacts on a regular basis; just to ensure they remain in top shape.

They invest hugely in insurance as a backup if any of the measures put in place are circumvented. Laws are also made to protect buildings, trees and other structures that have become National treasures!

Now, if people and organizations can go to these lengths to protect these "so called" important items, shouldn't we go even further to protect our hearts and minds?

Well, yes of course we should!

But the only way to achieve that is if we place even more value over our hearts and minds than these "so called" important items!

The good news is that you do not need to go looking for laser detectors, alarms, patrol guards, curators or insurance companies to guard your heart and mind. All you need is spelt out plainly in the Bible!

Let us see how the Bible provides the much-required protection for our hearts and minds.

For Laser Detectors and Alarms

Employ Word-based prayers; ask the Lord to probe your heart and examine your thoughts. The Word of God will detect any strays. Psalm 26:2 (NIV) says:

"Test me, Lord, and try me, examine my heart and my mind;

Also, Psalm 17:3a (NLT) says:

"You have tested my thoughts and examined my heart in the night. You have scrutinized me and found nothing wrong."

For Patrol Guards
Employ the Word of God; meditate on it and hide it in your heart.

Psalm 119:105 says:
"Thy word is a lamp unto my feet, and a light unto my path."

Also, Psalm 119:11 (KJV) says:
"Thy word have I hid in mine heart, that I might not sin against thee."

For Curators
Employ Word-based prayers; the Word of God has tremendous cleansing power. It is the same Word that Christ sanctified us by.
Ephesians 5:26 (KJV) says:
"That he might sanctify and cleanse it with the washing of water by the word,"
Psalm 51:7 (NIV) also says:
"Cleanse me with hyssop, and I will be clean; wash me, and I will be whiter than snow."

For Insurance
Build on the rock; by applying the Word of God in your life! It is a better guarantee than the offerings of any insurance company! Because after storm and barrage

against your heart and mind has come and gone, you will still remain standing!

Matthew 7:24-25 says:
"Everyone then who hears these words of mine and does them will be like a wise man who built his house on the rock. And the rain fell, and the floods came, and the winds blew and beat on that house, but it did not fall, because it had been founded on the rock."

For Laws
Need I say? Yes of course!
Many folks don't like to hear the word "law"; but laws are there to guard and guide us; God's laws fill us with wisdom and create boundaries that keep us safe from harm.

Proverbs 4:6 (TLB) says:
"Cling to wisdom — she will protect you. Love her — she will guard you."

Psalm 19:7a (NIV) says:
"The law of the Lord is perfect, refreshing the soul."

There you have it! The very first steps to guarding your hearts and minds.

As I wrap this introduction, I like to point out that God takes the state of our hearts and contents of our thoughts seriously and so should we!

In Genesis 11 when the people of the land came together to build a tower, God interrupted their plan. And in verse 6 the Lord said:

*". . . "Behold, they are one [unified] people, and they all have the same language. This is only the beginning of what they will do [in rebellion against Me], and now no evil thing they **imagine** they can do will be impossible for them." (AMP) Emphasis mine*

God also sent Lucifer packing from heaven because of the thoughts he harboured in his heart as we see in Isaiah 14:13-14

*"For **you said to yourself**, "I will ascend to heaven and rule the angels. I will take the highest throne. I will preside on the Mount of Assembly far away in the north. I will climb to the highest heavens and be like the Most High."" Emphasis mine*

The source of the words we speak is our hearts (minds) and Luke 6:45 tells us that:

*"The good man out of the good treasure of his **heart (mind)** brings forth what is good; and the evil man out of the evil*

*treasure brings forth what is evil; **for his mouth speaks from that which fills his heart.*** *Emphasis mine*

Proverbs 27:10 (NLT) says:
"As a face is reflected in water, so the heart reflects the real person."

I will like to welcome you to join me on yet another journey as we, through the pages of this book discover the requirements for guarding our hearts and minds!

In this journey, we will learn how to *value, guard* and ultimately *harness* the potentials God deposited in us through an understanding of the importance our hearts and minds play in determining the course of our lives! An understanding that will ultimately change our lives altogether for the better!

A Beautiful Place

S OMETIME AGO, I CAME ACROSS an interesting quote in "Today's Quote from God."

"The mind is a terribly dangerous place. Don't go in there without God."

Very interesting quote, I must say; Jeremiah 17:9 implies the same. And in Matt 15:17-20 Jesus said this of the heart:

"Do you not see that whatever goes into the mouth passes into the stomach and is expelled? **But what comes out of the mouth proceeds from the heart, and this defiles a person.** *For* **out of the heart** *come* **evil thoughts**, *murder, adultery, sexual immorality, theft, false witness, slander. These are what defile a person. But to eat with unwashed hands does not defile anyone."* Emphasis mine

You defile yourself by the words you speak and not what you eat; but what you speak comes from the thoughts formed based on the contents of you your heart. In Jeremiah 17:9 the Bible says that the heart of man is desperately wicked. However, originally, the mind was supposed to be a *"beautiful place"* and not a *"dangerous place."*

The mind God gave Adam and in effect, you and I in the Garden of Eden was beautiful! The Bible records that

when God wanted to name the animals, He brought them to Adam and whatever Adam called every living creature became their names; that is simply amazing!
His mind was operating on a divine plane! Pure, intelligent, innovative, insightful and wise!

Genesis 2:19-20a (KJV) gives the full account:
"And out of the ground the Lord God formed every beast of the field and every fowl of the air; and brought them unto Adam to see what he would call them: and **whatsoever Adam called every living creature that was the name thereof.** *And Adam gave names to all cattle, and to the fowl of the air, and to every beast of the field;"* Emphasis mine

The mind Adam and Eve had was without a doubt heavenly! I believe very strongly that they could also understand the language of the different animals! Why else did Eve not run away when the serpent spoke to her?
The same divine plane that Adam and Eve's mind operated on was what God's initial intention was for all our minds; nothing short of it! But then man sinned, and his mind became *"broken"* and perverted and consequently ours too.

Minds became troubled, sinful, blinded, depraved, dull and corrupt! We see the first result of this perversion in Cain's thinking. When in Genesis chapter 4 God did not accept Cain's offering, he became dejected and very angry and then plotted and killed his brother! (Genesis 4:3-8). And then in Genesis 6:5 during the time of Noah, the Bible says:

*"And God saw that the wickedness of man was great in the earth, and that every **imagination of the thoughts of his heart (mind)** was only evil continually." (KJV) Emphasis mine*

Starting from the fall of man, the minds of men continued to degenerate to the point that *every* *imagination* of the thoughts of their minds were *only* *evil continually!*

And over the years this persisted! Even after wiping out that generation, years after Noah and his family got off the ark, the depravity of the minds of men resurfaced again! (Genesis 19:4) and in verse 24, the Lord rained down fire from heaven and destroyed Sodom and Gomorrah.

It was one depravity after the other over the years that followed! But praise be to God that He did not leave our minds in that fallen state! He sent His only begotten Son to die in our stead and restore us!

Romans 5:15 (NLT) says:
"But there is a great difference between Adam's sin and God's gracious gift. For the sin of this one man, Adam, brought death to many. But even greater is God's wonderful grace and his

gift of forgiveness to many through this other man, Jesus Christ."

Christ's death and resurrection restored us and our minds back to operating on a divine plane!

So, I can confidently say that you have been blessed by God with *a beautiful mind* and we should treat our minds that way. 2 Timothy 2:20 (AMP) says:

"Now in a large house there are not only vessels and objects of gold and silver, but also vessels and objects of wood and of earthenware, and some are for honourable (noble, good) use and some for dishonourable (ignoble, common)."

This tells us that we would normally use the vessels of gold and silver for honourable purposes our minds should therefore be used for honourable and not dishonourable purposes. So, treat your mind as a vessel of honour and not like trash by letting trash dwell in it! That's why Paul was admonishing the Philippian church to think of things that are **true**, **noble**, and **just**.

Just in case you are having doubts, step in closer; let me *"introduce"* you to your heart and mind.

Your Heart is Special to God

It holds a special place in fulfilling your destiny in life; it is by your heart you are made right with God. That is

why it is very important to keep your heart with all diligence. Romans 10:10a says:
*"For it is by believing in your **heart** that you are made right with God,"*

Your Mind Is the Bedrock of Creativity
Creative thinking engages special parts of the brain to come up with innovative ideas. Trust the Lord to show you what you need to do! Exodus 35:30-33 tells of Bezalel whose mind was gifted with creativity.

"See, the Lord has called by name Bezalel the son of Uri, son of Hur, of the tribe of Judah; and he has filled him with the Spirit of God, with skill, with intelligence, with knowledge, and with all craftsmanship, to devise artistic designs, to work in gold and silver and bronze, in cutting stones for setting, and in carving wood, for work in every skilled craft."

Your Mind Is the Processor of Information.
It collates this information from our spirits souls and bodies. It is in a constant state of receiving and processing information all through our waking period. And even when we go to sleep it doesn't pack up for the day; the subconscious mind takes over the ***night shift*** and takes charge of our dreams, connecting them with the things we were engaged in during the day.

Romans 12:2 (TLB)

Chapter One: A Beautiful Place

*"Don't copy the behaviour and customs of this world, but be a new and different person with a fresh newness **in all you do and think. Then you will learn from your own experience** how his ways will really satisfy you." Emphasis mine*

Your Mind is Sound

The Spirit of God in us is One that gives us a sound and well-balanced mind; showing itself in a prudent conduct and behaviour; in moderation, self-control, purity, and honesty. 2 Timothy 1:7 (KJV) says:

*"For God hath not given us the spirit of fear; but of power, and of love, and of **a sound mind**." Emphasis mine*

Your Mind Is the Same as Christ's!

Amazing! Isn't it? To know this; that the mind we now have is that of Christ's, should get us all excited; but it is disheartening that we aren't. 1 Corinthians, 2:16 (AMP) says:

*"For who has known the mind and purposes of the Lord, so as to instruct Him? But **we have the mind of Christ** [to be guided by His thoughts and purposes]. Emphasis mine*

We know how we feel when we get compared with some earthly achiever; people take pride when they are tagged as some popular star's look alike, one celebrity or the other, etc. so here, the Bible says our minds are the same as Jesus' and we are not over the moon! We don't go all out to preserve that position . . . strange isn't it?

You and I have the mind of Christ; to think otherwise is a trick from the pit of hell! So, let's do all within our power to guard it, treat it honourably and keep it beautiful!

2

The Greatest Trick

THERE IS A POPULAR QUOTE from a 1995 mystery film titled: "The Usual Suspects"; that is very true today and has been for thousands of years:

"The greatest trick the devil ever pulled was convincing the world he didn't exist."

He is a trickster and a liar! That's why we need to be aware of his devices (2 Corinthians 2:11). There are many tricks up his sleeve; in this chapter, we will expose *some* of them.

Trick #1: The "I'm a Myth" Trick!
Billions of people today in the world have fallen victim of this trick! They have come to believe that the devil is only a myth made up by religions, story tellers and movie makers. It is quite an unfortunate situation, but it is because of what 2 Corinthians 4:4 (NIV) says. It says:

*"The god of this age **(the devil)** has **blinded the minds** of unbelievers, so that they **cannot see** the light of the gospel that displays the glory of Christ, who is the image of God." Emphasis mine*

Whether we are Christians or not; or whether we believe it or not, the devil and his agents are not fictional creatures; they are active in the world — corrupting men and women and causing them to turn away from God.

The devil has succeeded thus far because he has been able to perpetuate modern scepticism about the supernatural, including his own existence; causing even some godly people to let down their guard, and thereby becoming more vulnerable to his manipulations.

Trick #2: The "Be Scared" Trick!
The other trick he is constantly playing is the scare trick! Genesis 3:1 identifies him as being very crafty! He masks himself as a lion. In 1 Peter 5:8 the Bible says,
*"Be alert and of sober mind. Your enemy **the devil prowls around like a roaring** lion looking for someone to devour"*
Emphasis mine

Here we see that that the devil isn't a lion but prowls around like one! God is the Lion. Amos 3:8 says:
"The lion has roared who will not fear? The Sovereign Lord has spoken who can but prophesy?"

However, the devil goes ahead and roars like lions do that he might make his victims afraid. Scientists believe that when the lion sees its prey, it roars before it rushes on it; and that at this roaring many animals show great fear. The roar of a lion can paralyze its prey causing it to be an easy target.

If the devil can create fear in us, we become an easier prey for him to destroy. But that will not be our case; we are not unaware of his devices, so we won't be tricked!

James 4:7 implies that if we have submitted ourselves to the Lord we can resist the devil and he will flee from us! Jesus has also given us the authority to trample on snakes and scorpions and to overcome all the powers – *including the tricks* - of the enemy!

Trick #3: The "You are Helpless and Hopeless" Trick
With this trick, he uses people and situations to instil the helpless and hopeless belief in the minds of his victims. And once he's able to get into their minds this way he has them trapped, and he takes over the reins of their minds.

Gideon's story is an example of someone who had begun to see himself as helpless and hopeless. In Judges 6: 11 when the angel of the Lord visited him, he was beating wheat in the wine press instead of the threshing floor to hide it from the Midianites. And in verses 13 and 15, he revealed his hopelessness and helplessness.

*"13 Pardon me, my lord," Gideon replied, "but **if the Lord is with us, why has all this happened to us?** Where are all his wonders that our ancestors told us about when they said, 'Did not the Lord bring us up out of Egypt?' **But now the Lord has abandoned us** and given us into the hand of Midian." (NIV) Emphasis mine*

*"15 Pardon me, my lord," Gideon replied, "but how can I save Israel? **My clan is the weakest in Manasseh, and I am the least in my family."** (NIV) Emphasis mine*

The devil also makes people believe that it is impossible to live a sinless life; that to be holy is not possible and that **sin** is **acceptable**. That as long as we remain in this flesh **sin is in control and they're helpless.** "Let's be realistic" he says; "you can't be free of sin!" And I say that's a lie!
If it wasn't possible, God wouldn't request it from us. Peter in 1 Peter 1:16 quoted Leviticus 11:45b
". . . therefore you shall be holy, for I am holy."

Maybe you too have come to believe this is impossible. Well, you will soon discover otherwise!

Trick #4: The "Warped Consciousness" Trick
This is another subtle but very effective mind game he plays; especially on Believers.
He makes people conscious of things that wouldn't disturb his plans carefully wrapped in self-righteousness.
To be conscious is to be aware of, to be awake to and alive to something. He had the Pharisees trapped in the web of this subtle game of his and in their minds, they thought they were alright. In Matthew 23:23 Jesus rebuked the Scribes and Pharisees for not focusing on the things that really mattered.

*"Yes, woe upon you, Pharisees, and you other religious leaders—hypocrites! For you tithe down to the last mint leaf in your garden, **but ignore the important things—justice***

and mercy and faith. Yes, you should tithe, but you shouldn't leave the more important things undone."
(TLB) Emphasis mine

As long as the devil had them "distracted" he was fine. He also for instance, makes people sin conscious. So instead of them focusing on how to please God; they are focused on how to avoid sin!

From our definition of consciousness, it thus implies that to be sin conscious to be **aware of, awake to and alive to sin**! If you are always sin conscious it becomes a trap because you attract what you think. And this does not only apply to sin; it applies to both the negative and the positive! So why not focus on the positive?

Trick #5: The "Extremism" Trick
He has also mastered the art of extremism! For instance, the Bible teaches modesty and balance, but the devil incites extremes.
Proverbs 25:16 (AMP) says:
*"Have you found [pleasure sweet like] honey? **Eat only as much as you need**, otherwise, being filled excessively, you vomit it." Emphasis mine*

Romans 12:3 (AMP) says:
*"For by the grace [of God] given to me I say to everyone of you **not to think more highly of himself** [and of his importance and ability] **than he ought to think**; but to think so as to have*

sound judgment, as God has apportioned to each a degree of faith [and a purpose designed for service]." Emphasis mine

Ecclesiastes 7:18 (MSG) says:
*"It's best to **stay in touch with both sides of an issue**. A person who fears God deals responsibly with all of reality, **not just a piece of it**." Emphasis mine*

The reason he pushes his victims towards extremism is because he knows that anyone living at the "edge" is the one more likely to fall off the cliff!

In conclusion, we must remember that the devil is a trickster; and as it is with every trick; you walk away saying *"that can't be true!"*
And so it is; it isn't true!

So, here is what is true!
- *The devil isn't a myth! He only wants you to think he is!*
- *The devil isn't a lion! He only pretends to be; instead, he's a slimy old snake!*
- *You are not hopeless or helpless! He only wants you to believe that!*
- *You're no longer a slave to sin! You are a slave of righteousness!*
- *Balance and modesty is what the Bible teaches; not extremism!*

The Godly Thought Life

PAUL'S ADMONISHMENT IN Philippians 4:8 is geared towards us building a healthy and godly thought life. Because every single one of our actions originate from our thoughts. He first admonished us to fix our thoughts on that which is **true, good and right**.

These are the three core foundational blocks required for a godly thought life; *truth, goodness* and *righteousness*. It is very important to note that his admonishment is not to fix our thoughts on what is true, *or* good *or* right but **true and good and right**.

As lovely as having true, good or right thoughts are on their own; having each of them in isolation is not what the Bible admonishes. It is important to get all three together because not everything that is true is good and right. In addition, something can be true and good but not right.

For instance, (and I am being very broad here); it is **true** that in the world today people are defiling the laws of God. But defiling the laws of God is **not good** neither is it **right**.

When Ananias and Sapphirra sold a piece of land and brought only part of the money, claiming it was the full price; the gesture to sell was **good** but their presentation was **not true** and **right**

Eve saw that the fruit of the tree was **good** for food and pleasing to the eye, and that it was desirable for gaining wisdom . . . this was also **true**; but eating the fruit was not **right**!

Our actions are consequences of our thoughts; so, when we say things and do things that are true and good but mostly with the wrong motives; we are not doing what is right and pleasing to the Father. The "rightness" part stems solely from our motives; and you know God sees and judges our motives.

Let us therefore, fix our thoughts on that which is *true* and *good* and *right*! This is the foundation required for a godly thought life that makes the difference in anyone's life. Paul was admonishing the church in Philippi because he knew of the natural tendencies of the mind. Philippians 4:8 (KJV) admonishes:

*"Finally, brethren, whatever things are **true**, whatever things are **noble**, whatever things are **just**, whatever things are pure, whatever things are lovely, whatever things are of good report, if there is any virtue and if there is anything praiseworthy—meditate on these things." Emphasis mine*

The Living Bible renders this verse as thus:

*"And now, brothers, as I close this letter, let me say this one more thing: **Fix your thoughts** on what is **true** and **good** and **right**. Think about things that are pure and lovely, and dwell on the fine, good things in others. Think about all you can praise God for and be glad about." Emphasis mine.*

Fix your thoughts . . ..
"Fix my thoughts?"
"What? "
"Are you kidding me?"
"Have you met my thoughts?"
"My thoughts are as free as a bird!"
"They take up flight to the highest heights and free fall to the lowest depths. How in the world am I expected to fix my thoughts?"
Tough isn't it?

Obeying this command requires a conscious and deliberate effort. Because naturally, our thoughts tend to drift and sometimes into "uncontrolled" zones! Some of these "uncontrolled" thoughts are very easy to identify when they arrive, but some others are subtle, more cunning and even still, more dangerous. But you can, and you have the ability to choose what you think!

Many times, we have heard statements like: "I'm sorry, I shouldn't have said so and so; I wasn't thinking straight." This usually stems from *"thoughts that have a mind of their own!"* These thoughts constitute the thoughts Paul refers to in 2 Corinthians 10:5 (NKJV):

*"casting down arguments and every high thing that exalts itself against the knowledge of God, **bringing every thought into captivity to the obedience of Christ**" Emphasis mine*

To bring *every thought into captivity to the obedience of Christ* means we do anything it takes to bring the thought under control, to conquer and dethrone it from its acclaimed exalted place and bring it into submission under the rule and reign of Christ.

Jeremiah 17:9 (NIV) says:
*"The heart **(mind)** is deceitful above all things and beyond cure. Who can understand it?" Emphasis mine*

Once your thoughts are fixed (guided) by these foundational blocks; on what is good, true and right then you will be in pole position to think about things that are pure and lovely and dwell on the fine, good things in others! The Message version includes the following about others:
"- the best, not the worst; the beautiful, not the ugly; things to praise, not things to curse."

So, what are the things we think about?

You will agree that it is almost impossible to have a "blank" mind even when we are not actively engaged in thinking. But how do we occupy our minds especially when we are not actively engaged and get rid of "stray" thoughts?

One practice that will help in checking the things we think about is to ask yourself if you wouldn't mind if the thoughts you harboured in your mind were played in the church sound system during Sunday School or better still if they were converted into images and played out on your church projector on Sunday morning just before the message came.

Or if you wouldn't mind coming into the office or into the school and hearing your thoughts being played out in the public address system. Bottom line is this:

If you are not proud of your thoughts, then they have no business in your mind!

Psalm 24:3-4 says:

"Who shall ascend into the hill of the LORD? or who shall stand in his holy place? He that hath clean hands, and a pure heart; who hath not lifted up his soul unto vanity, nor sworn deceitfully. He shall receive the blessing from the LORD, and righteousness from the God of his salvation"

Once we have our thought lives aligned with being good, true and right then we wouldn't have any difficulty harbouring thoughts that are pure and lovely, these will come naturally! And so will dwelling on the fine, good things in others; not the ugly and bad things!

We will be able to see the good in people and embrace and encourage them to change instead of dwelling on their weaknesses! We wouldn't have any difficulty thinking about all we can praise God for and be glad about.

Before closing this chapter, we will consider how we can identify a godly thought life.

A godly thought life is guided by the Spirit of God
A godly thought life is a thought life that does not solely depend on the reasoning dictated by only our five senses but one that is guided by the Spirit.

"The mind governed by the flesh is death, but the mind governed by the Spirit is life and peace." Romans 8:6 (NIV).

The Spirit of God reveals to us the great things God has in store for us. 1 Corinthians 2:9 – 10 (NIV) says:

*"However, as it is written: "What no eye has seen, what no ear has heard, and what no human mind has conceived"—the things God has prepared for those who love him—**these are the things God has revealed to us by his Spirit**. The*

Spirit searches all things, even the deep things of God"
Emphasis mine

A godly thought life is having the mind of Christ

A godly thought life is ultimately having the mind of
Christ. 1Corinthians, 2:16 (AMP) says:
*"For who has known the mind and purposes of the Lord, so as
to instruct Him? But **we have the mind of Christ** [to be
guided by His thoughts and purposes]. Emphasis mine*

Having the mind of Christ is being able to think as He
thought. So how did Christ think? Let us consider just a
few we can pattern out thought lives after.

He Thought Humbly – Philippians 2:5-6 (MSG)

*"Think of yourselves the way Christ Jesus thought of himself.
He had equal status with God but didn't think so much of
himself that he had to cling to the advantages of that status no
matter what. Not at all."*

He Thought Compassionately - Matthew 9:36 (NIV)

*"When he saw the crowds, he had compassion on them,
because they were harassed and helpless, like sheep without a
shepherd."*

He Thought Confidently – John 10:30 (KJV)

"I and my Father are one."

A statement that without a doubt put Him the black books of the religious leaders of His day. He was not afraid but supremely confident. His confidence however, flowed from His humility. Jesus was confident in the Father; we can be confident in Him too. Our confidence should stem from our humility; trusting in God more than we do ourselves.

He Thought Purposefully – John 10:10b (AMP)
"I came that they may have and enjoy life, and have it in abundance (to the full, till it overflows)"

Seek your purpose in life and channel your thought and energy towards achievement of such purpose. A life without purpose is a wasted life.

Our Thoughts Impact Our Behaviour

THE WAY WE THINK WILL naturally influence our conversation. It also impacts our behavior and ultimately who we are!
This is how it works scientifically; thoughts stimulate electrochemical responses, which produces emotions; emotions result in attitudes; and attitudes produce behaviours.
This is how the Bible puts it in Proverbs 23:7 (NKJV):
"For as he thinks in his heart, so is he."

It is very important that we guard the way we think, and what we think about. Because the way we think inadvertently influences the way we live. We must therefore fill our minds with the right thoughts.
This means desisting from meditating on evil, impure and immoral thoughts or "excessively" on what we have done, wrong; because it keeps our minds on the negative. Instead we should centre our thoughts on Christ, on good, positive, excellent and righteous thoughts!

The thoughts that come to our minds are either natural or unnatural. Our natural thoughts stem from the exterior, our environment and associations and the elements that form our thoughts find their way into our minds by our senses. Through the things we see; the things we hear, and what we smell, touch and taste. These senses send signals to our brains for processing and the mind uses the processed information to form our thoughts. These natural thoughts can either be positive or negative based on what we have seen and how we perceived and interpreted them.

Unnatural thoughts on the other hand are influenced by external but unseen "forces"; either good or bad, and they can either be positive or negative too.

Positively "influenced" thoughts come from God. The Bible says in Jeremiah 31:33

*"This is the covenant I will make with the people of Israel after that time," declares the LORD. "**I will put my law in their minds and write it on their hearts**. I will be their God, and they will be my people" Emphasis mine.*

Ezekiel 36:26 (KJV) also says:
"A new heart also will I give you, and a new spirit will I put within you: and I will take away the stony heart out of your flesh, and I will give you an heart of flesh."

Negatively "influenced" thoughts come from the devil Matthew 12: 22-23a (AMP) says:

"Peter took Him aside [to speak to Him privately] and began to reprimand Him, saying, "May God forbid it! This will

never happen to You." But Jesus turned and said to Peter, "Get behind Me, Satan!"

See also James 3:14-16
*"But **if ye have bitter envying and strife in your hearts,** glory not, and lie not against the truth. This wisdom descendeth not from above, **but is earthly, sensual, devilish.**" Emphasis mine.*

Having seen the origins and effects of positive and negative thoughts, it is vital therefore that because we become what we think; we focus our thoughts on **our potentials**, not **our limitations**; and meditate on our strengths not our weaknesses.

This principle of becoming what you think is easily seen in our world today. You can easily tell the difference between the person who applies Philippians 4:8 from the one who doesn't. The fruits are obvious!

Jesus said in Matt. 7:20 (NLT)

"Yes, just as you can identify a tree by its fruit, so you can identify people by their actions."

A while ago I was in the company of a few brothers as we were preparing for our annual outreach program and a brother shared a joke with us. He said a certain pastor was asked what the numerical strength of his congregation was, and his answer was: *"we are under*

2000." They later found out that he only had 19 members! At first, we all laughed and then started to analyze his response.

Firstly, we all agreed that his response wasn't a lie! 19 is under 2000! We joked about it and swung his response back and forth. And concluded that he was playing mind games; leaving too much to the imagination!

2 Corinthians 1:13 (MSG) admonishes
"Don't try to read between the lines or look for hidden meanings in this letter. **We're writing plain, unembellished truth,** *hoping that you'll now see the whole picture as well as you've seen some of the details."* *Emphasis mine*

Unlike Paul, this individual wasn't offering plain or unembellished truth; as a matter of fact, he was offering the exact opposite! Deliberately manipulating people to "read between the lines" leaving room for them to interpret or misinterpret. The Bible in Matthew 5:37 says let your nay be nay and yea, yea! When you leave too much to the imagination, you are more likely to deceive your audience. The Message version of the Bible puts it thus:

"Just say 'yes' and 'no.' when you manipulate words to get your own way, you go wrong"

If your thought life borders around grey areas, your behaviour will likewise be around those fringes and ultimately your lifestyle. And unless you are a dubious person, you wouldn't want to live your life bordering around grey areas. The chorus of a song titled "Slow Fade" by Casting Crowns says:

"It's a slow fade when you give yourself away
*It's a slow fade **when black and white have turned to grey***
Thoughts invade, choices are made, a price will be paid
When you give yourself away
People never crumble in a day. . ."

Once we allow our hearts and minds; the "control room" of life's outcomes gravitate towards grey areas, we are toiling with trouble because this "control room" *controls* what we become! This brings us back to Proverbs 23:7; our mantle scripture for this chapter which says:

"For as he thinks in his heart, so is he."

So, if your heart harbours evil, your mind will naturally gravitate towards sinful thoughts and ultimately, you become sinful in nature and if you are dominated by the sinful nature you can only think about sinful things. And you find you are locked in an unending cycle of darkness, evil and sin!
Romans 8:5-6 (NLT) says

*"**Those who are dominated by the sinful nature think about sinful things,** but those who are controlled by the Holy Spirit think about things that please the Spirit. So letting your sinful nature control your mind leads to death. But letting the Spirit control your mind leads to life and peace." Emphasis mine*

The call now is for you to step *your mind* out of the *darkness*, the *greys* and the *shadows* into the marvelous light of the Saviour and watch your behaviour and consequently your life change from glory to glory!

The Mind Game

THE MIND IS A BATTLEGROUND! A battleground where forces of darkness are waging war to take over control by any and every means necessary. This battle is not just for the Christian alone but also for everyone! The devil works upon the mind because he knows once he has control of the mind of a person; he has control of that person. The only way we can win the battle is if we channelled our thoughts appropriately.

Romans 7:23 tells us about this war:
*"But there is another power within me that is **at war with my mind**. This power makes me a slave to the sin that is still within me."* Emphasis mine

Everyone is in this battle; and like in every battle, the landscape of the battleground covers a broad spectrum of the warring parties, victors and victims! There are human agents knowingly and unknowingly pushing the agenda of the devil; they are warring against the saints of God and the Gospel of truth. There are also those (unaware of the battle), who have been taken captive by the devil and his agents and have become slaves to sin. There are more importantly those who have encountered the truth and have become victorious!

Chapter Five: The Mind Game

Sometime ago, while doing a book study of "The Believer's Authority"; a book written by Kenneth E. Hagin during our midweek Bible Study in church, we learnt a very vital truth.

"That we should not engage the devil in his domain- the domain of reason!"

Because he is crafty and the father of all lies and we cannot win the battle in this domain! Instead, we should take the battle to the domain of faith! Where the Believer's authority can be exercised; and the devil is left confused!

John 8:44b says of him:

"He has always hated the truth because there is no truth in him. When he lies, it is consistent with his character; for he is a liar and the father of lies"

He is a "twister" of the truth and the number one protagonist of extremes! He conned Eve into disobeying God by twisting the truth because Eve in the first place gave him audience trying to debate with him in the place of reason. It all started with his subtle suggestions; pushing the question to the extreme:

"Did God really say, 'You must not eat from any tree in the garden'? "Emphasis mine

Moments later the woman was eating the fruit and giving her husband to eat!

The Devil attacks us mainly through our thoughts, not because he knows what we are thinking but because he can suggest to us what to think. Once he knows he has us thinking his own thoughts; by the words we speak and actions we take; he has the opportunity then to manipulate us. He introduces worry, grief, anxiety, and fear; waging a constant attack on our spirits and our minds.

In this next section, in accordance with the Bible's admonishment about us not being ignorant of the devil's devices, I will be drawing our attention to some of his well-disguised *"crafts"* that he has being deploying over the ages; in the lives of many. Believers have not been exempted from his antics.

1. The Misdirected Obedience Antic

The first we will consider, and what I believe to be his craftiest move ever, is making *even* Christians "obey" God for the wrong reasons!

How do I mean?

Many of us obey God because of the *fear* of the consequences of disobedience instead of obeying Him out of *love!* However, 1 John 5:3 (NIV) says:

"In fact, this is love for God: to keep his commands. And his commands are not burdensome,"

I do not trust in God's grace to live a sinless life because I am afraid of going to hell, but I trust in God's grace to live a sinless life because I am on my way to heaven!

Once he gets people to "obey" God out of fear he puts them in a place of constant struggle.
1 John 4:16-18 (TLB) says:

"We know how much God loves us because we have felt his love and because we believe him when he tells us that he loves us dearly. God is love, and anyone who lives in love is living with God and God is living in him. And as we live with Christ, our love grows more perfect and complete; so, we will not be ashamed and embarrassed at the day of judgment, but can face him with confidence and joy because he loves us and we love him too. We need have no fear of someone who loves us perfectly; his perfect love for us eliminates all dread of what he might do to us. If we are afraid, it is for fear of what he might do to us and shows that we are not fully convinced that he really loves us"

2. The Erroneous Thinking Antic
He keeps people trapped with the wrong thinking and a false mentality; that they are not good enough, that

they are in the wrong bodies, that they cannot be free, that they cannot get better, and with this lie, he has locked many onto the slave mentality like the children of Israel. He makes them believe the lies he's fed to them through his numerous agents in the world; misguided, superficial and outright ignorant people, streaming lies through his negatively influenced policies, all forms of media, etc. and so many people have believed his lies and have lied to themselves so long that they have lost the capacity for the truth. 1 Timothy 4:2 (MSG) says:

"These liars have lied so well and for so long that they've lost their capacity for truth."

John 8:32 (KJV) says:
"And ye shall know the truth, and the truth shall make you free."

The flip side of this scripture holds true too.
"But if you believe a lie, that lie will have you bound"

Just like the encounter of the spies in Numbers 13:33 who believed the lie of the enemy and came back from spying the land thinking they were grasshoppers!

"There we saw the Nephilim (the sons of Anak are part of the Nephilim); **and we were like grasshoppers in our own sight***, and so we were in their sight." (AMP) Emphasis mine*

He is even able to then drive people mad and to the point of suicide. To the outside world, you hear phrases like **"the person just snapped"**
Well, we know better!
Psalm 139:14 tells us that we fearfully and wonderfully made and that God's works are marvelous! Genesis 1:31 tells us the same.

"God saw everything that He had made, and behold, it was very good and He validated it completely." (AMP)

3. The Double Minded State Antic
Another "game" he plays is that of doubt and unbelief. He keeps even well-meaning Believers in the double-minded state. This is a very dangerous and wasteful state to be as a Believer. See what the Bible says in James Chapter 1

Verse 6: **"the one who doubts is like a wave of the sea, blown and tossed by the wind"**

Then in Verse 8, that such a person **"is unstable in all his ways."**

Verse 7 tells us the outcome of such people.

*"Such people should not expect to receive **anything** from the Lord." (NLT) Emphasis mine*

4. The "Guilt and Condemnation Card" Antic

Finally, he plays the "guilt and condemnation card." Once he has succeeded in causing his victim to sin against God, he turns around and throws guilt and condemnation at them! However, the Bible tells us in Romans 8:1 that:

"There is therefore now no condemnation to them which are in Christ Jesus, who walk not after the flesh, but after the Spirit."

The Bible also tells us that he is the accuser of the brethren. Rev.12:10 says:

"And I heard a loud voice saying in heaven, now is come salvation, and strength, and the kingdom of our God, and the power of his Christ: for the accuser of our brethren is cast down, which accused them before our God day and night."

He plants his seeds (thoughts) in the minds of people and then uses those seeds as legal grounds for control, manipulation and condemnation.

In John 14:30 Jesus addressing His disciples said:

Chapter Five: The Mind Game

"Hereafter I will not talk much with you: for the prince of this world cometh, **and hath nothing; no power over, no hold on, and nothing to use against me.***" Emphasis mine*

The Mind Game Reloaded

T HERE IS ABSOLUTELY NOTHING the devil uses that he created! He has only mastered the art of twisting things and taking things to the extreme!

Therefore, in this chapter I invite you to turn the table against him too, using what the Creator Himself put inside of us - *obedience!*

The devil wants you to think you are nobody and that you are not important and like the other ten spies in Numbers 13:33 who saw themselves as grasshoppers that you are inconsequential but that is a lie! I say it is a lie because in fact:

You are a god!
Truth is Believers are not ordinary! This is what Psalm 82:6 says of you:
"I have said, ye are gods; and all of you are children of the Most High."

You Are a Partaker of God's Divine Nature!
That is what 2 Peter 1:4a (KJV) says:
*"Whereby are given unto us exceeding great and precious promises: that **by these ye might be partakers of the divine nature**," Emphasis mine*

You Have Escaped the Corruption of This World!
2 Peter 1:4b tells us this

"Having escaped the corruption that is in the world through lust."

You Are Fearfully and Wonderfully Made!
That is what Psalm 139:14 says
"I will praise thee; for I am fearfully and wonderfully made: marvellous are thy works; and that my soul knoweth right well."

You Are a Very Important Person!
1 Peter 3: 18 (AMP) says:
"For indeed Christ died for sins once for all, the Just and Righteous for the unjust and unrighteous [the Innocent for the guilty] so that He might bring us to God, having been put to death in the flesh, but made alive in the Spirit;"

We have seen aides take bullets for their presidents, kings, rulers, etc. they do this because of the importance they have placed on these leaders. You are very important; so important that not just anyone died for you but the King of kings!

Now that we have this sorted, let us show the devil who is the boss! Because we have authority over him and his cohorts. To do this, we need to see a couple of things differently!
Firstly, God can use even the devil as a tool!

Paul the Apostle had to change his thinking and attitude towards his weaknesses; and once he did that, he turned the joke on the devil.

In 2 Corinthians 12, we read of Paul talking about being given a weakness or limitation so that he will not get a "big head" because of the great revelations he had seen. As a matter of fact, it was Satan's angel that was given the task to get Paul down. As a human being he resisted the discomfort he felt by this and did not see anything good in it initially; so, he begged God to remove this discomfort. Once, twice, thrice and what did he get in response? 2 Corinthians 12:9 (KJV)

". . . My grace is sufficient for thee: for my strength is made perfect in weakness."

As soon as Paul heard this, his attitude to the discomfort changed when he realized that (this weakness was an avenue for Christ's strength to move into his life!) and that it was for his benefit! So, he accepted it with gladness, he changed his initial perception of it as an "evil limitation" and started appreciating it as a gift!

With this change in attitude, he began to take limitations in his stride, and with good cheer, these limitations that cut him down to size—abuse, accidents, opposition, etc. In verses 9b – 10 (KJV), he said:

Chapter Six: The Mind Game Reloaded

*"**Most gladly therefore will I rather glory in my infirmities**, that the power of Christ may rest upon me. Therefore, I take pleasure in infirmities, in reproaches, in necessities, in persecutions, in distresses for Christ's sake: **for when I am weak, then am I strong.** Emphasis mine*

He simply allowed Jesus Christ to take over! Instead of grumbling, complaining and speaking negatively about his weakness, Paul turned the joke on the devil! He turned to the Lord for strength each time; and so, the weaker the devil intended him to be, the stronger he became! Awesome!

I can imagine the confusion on the devil's face working tirelessly to weaken Paul but every day he sees the Apostle growing stronger and stronger!

Paul could defeat the devil in his weakness, because he knew how to turn the tables! Here are a few other biblical ways to do this

1. Change The Narrative!
The first way we will look at in turning the table against the devil is found in the book of Joel 3:10. It says:

*"Beat your plowshares into swords and your pruninghooks into spears: **let the weak say, I am strong.**" Emphasis mine*

The MSG version of puts it this way:
"Turn your shovels into swords; turn your hoes into spears. **Let the weak one throw out his chest and say, "I'm tough, I'm a fighter."** *Emphasis mine*

In other words, turn every supposed "disadvantage" to an "advantage"! Say what you want and not what you see or feel by faith!

2. Overcome Evil with Good
Jesus' teaching in Matthew 5:38-44 lists out several ways we can turn the table on the devil.

"You have heard that it was said, 'Eye for eye, and tooth for tooth.' **But I tell you, do not resist an evil person. If anyone slaps you on the right cheek, turn to them the other cheek also. And if anyone wants to sue you and take your shirt, hand over your coat as well. If anyone forces you to go one mile, go with them two miles.** *Give to the one who asks you, and do not turn away from the one who wants to borrow from you. "You have heard that it was said, 'Love your neighbour and hate your enemy.' But I tell you,* **love your enemies and pray for those who persecute you**"

Again, this will send confusion to the enemy's camp! His plan for evil is for you to drop your guard and take God's place as the One who metes out vengeance but instead of taking revenge on evil, you overcome it with good!

3. Do A Countdown Not a Count Out!

Carman wrote a song a couple of years ago about a fictitious battle between Jesus and Satan at Calvary; let me share a part of the narrated bit of the song with you:

"Then a Persona, yes, Extraordinaire appeared in centre ring.
God the Father will oversee the duel.
Opening the Book of Life, each grandstand hushed in awe as majestically He said,
"Now here's the rules.
He'll be wounded for their transgressions, bruised for iniquities"
When He said, "By His stripes they're healed," the devil shook!
He screamed, "Sickness is my specialty. I hate that healing junk!"
God said, "You shut your face, I wrote the book!"

Then the Father looked at His Only Son and said,
"You know the rules.
Your blood will cleanse their sin and calm their fears."
Then He pointed His finger at Satan and said,
"And I know you know the rules.
You've been twisting them to deceive My people for years."
Satan cried, "I'll kill you Christ! You'll never win this fight!"

The demons wheezed, "That's right, there ain't no way."
Satan jeered, "You're dead meat, Jesus, I'm gonna bust you up tonight!"
Jesus said, "Go ahead, make my day!"

The bell, the crowd, the fight was on,
And the devil leaped in fury.
With all his evil tricks he came undone.
He threw his jabs of hate and lust, a stab of pride and envy.
But the hands that knew no sin blocked every one.

Forty days and nights they fought, and Satan couldn't touch Him.
Now the final blow saved for the final round.
Prophetically Christ's hands came down
And Satan struck in vengeance!
The blow of death felled Jesus to the ground.
The devils roared in victory!
The saints shocked and perplexed as wounds appeared upon His hands and feet.
Then Satan kicked Him in His side, and blood and water flowed.
And they waited for 'The 10-count of defeat'.

God the Father turned His head,
His tears announcing Christ was dead!
The 10-count would proclaim the battle's end.

Then Satan trembled through his sweat in unexpected horror, yet...

As God started to count by saying,
"...10..."
"Hey wait a minute, God..."
"...9..."
"Stop! You're counting wrong..."
"...8..."
"His eyes are moving..."
"...7..."
"His fingers are twitching..."
"...6..."
"Where's all this Light coming from?"
"...5..."
"He's alive!"
"...4..."
"Oh - nooooo!"
"...3..."
"Oh...Yessssss!"
"...2..."
He has won!
"...1..."
He has won!
He's alive forevermore!
He is risen, He is Lord,

Interesting concept about the count. It was not a count out but a countdown! A count out is to end a battle but a countdown is to commence something! Never count yourself out; whenever the enemy wants you to do that; turn the tables on him and countdown instead!

1 Corinthians 2:8 (NIV) says:
"None of the rulers of this age understood it, for if they had, ***they would not have crucified the Lord of glory.*** *"*
Emphasis mine

This goes to show us the limitations of the devil; he was completely ignorant of God's intention, but the Father reveals His intentions to us!

1 Corinthians 2:10a (NIV) says:
"these are the things God has revealed to us by his Spirit."

Of course, the devil will win every ***mind game*** you play in his domain. Therefore, you need to turn the tables against him and move the battle away from the domain of ***reason (mind games),*** to the domain of faith ***(faith games)*** and watch him scamper off tail between his legs!

Thought Influencers

B EFORE I GO INTO THIS CHAPTER I will like to share with you the full lyrics of the song by Casting Crowns called "Slow Fade" that I mentioned briefly in Chapter Four.

Verse 1
Be careful little eyes what you see
It's the second glance that ties your hands as darkness pulls the strings
Be careful little feet where you go
For it's the little feet behind you that are sure to follow

Chorus
It's a slow fade when you give yourself away
It's a slow fade when black and white have turned to grey
Thoughts invade, choices are made, a price will be paid
When you give yourself away
People never crumble in a day
It's a slow fade, it's a slow fade

Verse 2
Be careful little ears what you hear
When flattery leads to compromise, the end is always near
Be careful little lips what you say
For empty words and promises lead broken hearts astray

Bridge
The journey from your mind to your hands

Is shorter than you're thinking
Be careful if you think you stand
You just might be sinking

Chorus 2
It's a slow fade when you give yourself away
It's a slow fade when black and white have turned to grey
Thoughts invade, choices are made, a price will be paid
When you give yourself away
People never crumble in a day
Daddies never crumble in a day
Families never crumble in a day

Outro
Oh be careful little eyes what you see
Oh be careful little eyes what you see
For the Father up above is looking down in love
Oh be careful little eyes what you see

"People never crumble in a day! it's a slow fade."

Your environment affects the way you think. We have learnt that the mind is the processor of information. It collates information from our spirits, souls and bodies. The verses of this song make mention of the factors that I believe affect the way we think. No harm in giving it a second read; so, go ahead and pay close attention to the consequences of each action.

Okay, let us have a close look at them

1. The Things We See
"Be careful little eyes what you see
It's the second glance that ties your hands as darkness
pulls the strings"

It is the second glance that ties your hands as darkness pulls the strings! Awesome! The first glance is the bait and "darkness" lurks around waiting if you will cast a second; and while it waits, it injects thoughts about what you have just seen hoping you will look again. With a second glance, the thoughts come rushing like a flood to overpower you!

Psalm 101:3a (NLT) says:
"I will refuse to look at anything vile and vulgar."

Job 31:1 (NLT) says:
"I made a covenant with my eyes not to look lustfully at a young woman."

Be careful about what you watch on television, on the Internet and social media because what we see affects the way we think either positively or negatively.

The Positive
For instance, God needed to change Abraham's mind set so He asked him to look at the stars in the sky.

Chapter Seven: Thought Influencers

Genesis 15:5 (NIV) says:
"He took him outside and said, "Look up at the sky and count the stars--if indeed you can count them." Then he said to him, "So shall your offspring be."

The Negative

One day, David stumbles into a scene that he could not take his eyes off; he thinks about what he had just seen for a while, commits himself, falls into sin and tries to cover his sin by having Uriah come from battle, go home, relax and perhaps "sleep with" his wife. 2 Samuel 11:2-5 (TLB)

"One night he couldn't get to sleep and went for a stroll on the roof of the palace. As he looked out over the city, he noticed a woman of unusual beauty taking her evening bath. He sent to find out who she was and was told that she was Bathsheba, the daughter of Eliam and the wife of Uriah. Then David sent for her and when she came he slept with her. (She had just completed the purification rites after menstruation.) Then she returned home. When she found that he had gotten her pregnant she sent a message to inform him."

The entire episode ended in murder. David did not start with the intention of committing murder; it was just the momentary pleasure of "stolen bread"; and then, deception. "A simple deception would do no one harm", he must have thought. But see how thesituation spiralled out of control?

Luke 11:34 (TLB) says:
" *Your eyes light up your inward being. A pure eye lets sunshine into your soul. A lustful eye shuts out the light and plunges you into darkness.*

We have seen how what we see can yield either positive or negative results. So why don't we focus on the positive instead of the self-destruct path the devil offers? We see how God helped Abraham create a mental image of his blessings we should therefore create images of success, freedom, joy, peace, etc. in our minds and keep visualizing them!

The Bible says of our Heavenly Father in Romans 4:17b (NIV):
"--the God who gives life to the dead and calls into being things that were not."

2. The Things We Hear
"Be careful little ears what you hear
When flattery leads to compromise, the end is always near"
1 Samuel 18, David got enrolled in Saul's army, and he became very successful. Saul saw that David was committed, diligent and efficient and rewarded him

accordingly. Soon afterwards, in verses 7-8 he lost the plot and became cynical when he **heard** people acknowledging David's achievements. In verse 8, we detect the cause of this change – jealousy and insecurity.

"As they danced, they sang: "Saul has slain his thousands, and David his tens of thousands." Saul was very angry; this refrain displeased him greatly. "They have credited David with tens of thousands," he thought, "but me with only thousands. What more can he get but the kingdom?" And from that time on Saul kept a close eye on David."

Luke 8:18 (TLB) says:
*"Therefore, **consider carefully how you listen**. Whoever has will be given more; whoever does not have, even what they think they have will be taken from them." Emphasis mine*

It is not only flattery we should be wary of but gossip as well! Because Proverbs 18:8 (AMP) says

*"The words of a whisperer (gossip) are like dainty morsels [to be greedily eaten]; **They go down into the innermost chambers** of the body [to be remembered and mused upon]."*

The words go into the heart; to be pondered upon and before you know it the thought becomes overwhelming!

3. The Places We Go
"Be careful little feet where you go
For it's the little feet behind you that are sure to follow"
This is an interesting one because our wrong choices can lead those who look up to us for direction astray. Remember what Jesus said about those who lead the little ones astray? (See Matt. 18:6)
Our physical senses collect the things we feel from our environments; the things we touch, taste and smell! Our senses serve as "collectors"; they collect information from the outside world and dump them in our minds for "processing"
The thoughts we permit into our minds do not stay idly there! As soon as they get in they begin to work either positively improving our health or negatively; eating away like the metastasis of cancer!

Proverbs 17:22 says:
"A cheerful heart does good like medicine, but a broken spirit makes one sick."

What David felt that night on the roof of the palace; affected his reasoning and led him on a downward spiral; from the rooftop to a sack of ashes! When a God-fearing person encounters any ill, the initial feeling is that of uneasiness. This feeling of discomfort should be taken as a signal to escape immediately and not linger.

4. The Things We Say
"Be careful little lips what you say
For empty words and promises lead broken hearts astray"
The effect of the things we say is like a double-edged sword! They can destroy the hearts and minds of others on the one hand and destroy ours on the other. Therefore, we should be careful of the things we say to others and even more importantly the things we say to and of ourselves!

Remember that life and death are in the power of our tongues! Proverbs 18:21(NLT) says:

"The tongue can bring death or life; those who love to talk will reap the consequences."

The things we say affect our environments and our environments affect the way we think! So, pay close attention to your utterances and keep always positive! Proverbs 11:11 (MSG) says:

"When right-living people bless the city, it flourishes;
evil talk turns it into a ghost town in no time. *Emphasis mine*

After the spies gave their negative report to the people, they raised a lament as we see in Numbers 14:1-2 (TLB)

*"Then all the people began weeping aloud and they carried on all night. Their voices rose in a great chorus of complaint against Moses and Aaron. **"We wish we had died in Egypt," they wailed, "or even here in the wilderness"** Emphasis mine*

Then, God himself answered them in verse 28 (KJV):

*"Say unto them, as truly as I live, saith the LORD, **as ye have spoken in mine ears, so will I do to you:"***

And they surely died in the wilderness as they said; every single one of them belonging to that generation except for Joshua and Caleb. As we see in Numbers 32:12-13 (NIV)

"not one except Caleb son of Jephunneh the Kenizzite and Joshua son of Nun, for they followed the LORD wholeheartedly. The LORD's anger burned against Israel and he made them wander in the wilderness forty years, until the whole generation of those who had done evil in his sight was gone."

In concluding this chapter about the things that influence our thoughts, let me draw your attention once again to the chorus of the song:

Chapter Seven: Thought Influencers

It's a slow fade when you give yourself away
It's a slow fade when black and white have turned to grey
Thoughts invade, choices are made, a price will be paid
When you give yourself away
People never crumble in a day. . .

Handling the Sin Stronghold

NOT MANY PEOPLE IN THIS WORLD enjoy being slaves to sin. I say "not many" because there are a good number of people in the world today who enjoy being slaves to sin! The reason, unknown to them, however, is ignorance. They actually think they are having a great time!

I also know of many people who really want to change the way they live and be able to live *above* sin, and to be free from bad habits and other addictions that are destroying their physical, mental and emotional lives; but they are unable to let go. And even though Romans 6:14 (NIV) says:

"For sin shall no longer be your master, because you are not under the law, but under grace."
Such people still find themselves slaves to sin!

To live above sin, we need to guard our thoughts because there is no sin that is committed that does not originate from our hearts and minds! In fact, all sin begins in our hearts and minds!

In Mark 7:20-23, Jesus said,
"That which proceeds out of the man that is what defiles the man. For from within, out of the heart of men, proceed the evil thoughts, fornications, thefts, murders, adulteries, deeds of coveting and wickedness, as well as deceit, sensuality, envy,

*slander, pride and foolishness. **All these evil things proceed from within and defile the man**" Emphasis mine*

No one commits these outward sins without first having committed them inwardly. Therefore, if we want to grow in godliness, we must win the battle over sin on the thought level.

We all have areas of vulnerability, which, if not disciplined by character and commitment, have the potential to defeat or even destroy us. The Bible says,

"Each one is tempted when he is drawn away by his own [particular] desires and enticed" (James 1:14 NKJV).

To be tempted by a thought entering the mind is not a sin. However, when we dwell upon that evil thought and allow it to **"draw us away"** and we then begin to wallow in it, that is when we sin.

Checking a thought against the three basic paths of – **truth, goodness** and **righteousness** once it enters our minds will help determine if we discard the thought or not.
The best practice is to deal with the thought as soon as it comes knocking because it naturally becomes harder to deal with when we allow a thought gain grounds in our hearts and minds.

You may be struggling with a weakness that has you chained down! Stuck in a vicious never-ending cycle. Up one day and down the other. Every fibre of your being wants to let go of this "weight" like Hebrews 12:1 admonishes but it is overwhelming:

"Therefore, since we are surrounded by such a huge crowd of witnesses to the life of faith, let us strip off every weight that slows us down, especially the sin that so easily trips us up. And let us run with endurance the race God has set before us." (NLT)

Many have tried so very hard to lay aside their weakness for days, weeks, months and perhaps years even; but have failed. Now they have become sceptical; and when they hear people say they are free from sin; they doubt the possibility. Can you identify with that? Well, you are not alone!

To be tempted is not a sin; but it is yielding to the temptation that is! Jesus Christ Himself was led to the wilderness by the Holy Spirit to be **tempted** by the devil. So, you are not alone there! However, if you find yourself constantly thinking about sin, and the guilts of the past you will live your life guilt-ridden and stuck in the past. However, if you switch your thoughts to how you have been liberated by the law of the Spirit of life in Christ Jesus, you will be free from the control and manipulation of the devil! The reason is not far-fetched. Whatever you keep your mind on (think about often) will affect your whole being.

Let me explain this based on modern day technology. Sin is like a tracking device that the devil uses to *monitor* his own. But this device does not only serve as a monitoring device it also allows for *remote control* and *manipulation.*

To be able to control its host remotely, the tracking device needs to be connected to a power source. Just like how electronic devices are powered remotely using power over Ethernet, sin is powered by junk thoughts of the mind!

Therefore, to render sin useless, rid it of its power by starving it of junk thinking! After a while, it will no longer have a "live connection" and become useless in your life!

Here is another analogy drawn from computing technology. Sin is like a "backdoor"

A backdoor in software or a computer system is a means (mostly undocumented) that allows an administrator to access a computer system or encrypted data bypassing the system's customary security mechanisms. It also refers to a secret portal that hackers and intelligence agencies use to gain illicit access.

In the same vein, sin serves as a backdoor that the devil uses to gain control of people's thoughts for manipulation and control!

Having a clear understanding and appropriate revelation, on how to handle the sin stronghold is the key to living victoriously. Otherwise, the norm would be struggling with sin, day in, day out, stumbling, falling, rising, and falling again!

I know this because I have been there before. Until one day I *"caught the revelation"* to live above sin! God, by His grace taught me what I needed to know.

First, He made me realize that the loophole in my life that kept me slave to my struggles were the thoughts I entertained in my mind! These thoughts; injected by demonic forces would becloud good and righteous judgement blinding me from the truth I know. Then like a lamb led to the slaughter, drag me out from the place of grace; and now helpless I cede to sin's pressure. Then once it is over, the demonic forces would retreat, and the thoughts would disappear. But on their way out, they would replace the thoughts with a feeling of guilt and helplessness!

He opened the eyes of my understanding to the grace that I should key into – *the one that enables me to control the thoughts my mind entertained;* and I finally saw the *way of escape that the Lord made* and have since continued to use it as a means of escape when temptation comes!

To see tried, tested and trusted ways you too can employ to live above sin! Jump ahead to chapter 14: ***Ten Powerhouse Protocols***.

The purpose of these chapters is to strengthen you! Because you too can be free from sin's stronghold!

Here's what God told Cain in Genesis 4:7 (TLB); and this is very vital to us as Believers. We can conquer sin!

"But if you refuse to obey, watch out. Sin is waiting to attack you, longing to destroy you. ***But you can conquer it!"***
Emphasis mine

The Place of Grace

I T IS ONLY JUST APT THAT after talking about handling the stronghold of sin we talk about the place of grace. Because by now it is natural that the question about where grace comes into play may be ringing in your mind. Right?

One of the greatest weapons God has given Believers in this life is His grace! It opens doors for us, lifts us up, changes situations for the better, rescues us from sin's hold, and the list goes on and on.

Oh, the amazing things grace can do! Because to experience grace is to experience God Himself stepping into your situation and lending a helping hand even though we do not deserve it!

It is also one of the Father's blessings that has been seriously misconstrued and abused.

Before we look at the place grace in transforming our lives especially over the stronghold of sin, first, we will consider what grace is not and what it does not do.

Grace is not an excuse to sin and does not necessarily prevent consequence. Many of us expect that when we commit sin, grace should "cover" our sins. God is not interested in disgracing us; so, most of the time if we are quick to repent, we are saved the embarrassment of being "found out".

The truth however is that it does not work that way all the time. God, by His grace can forgive our sins but we may still get to live with the consequences of our actions.

Chapter Nine: The Place of Grace

To drive home my point, I would like to share a very short *fictitious* scenario:

"A well-known and respected married brother sleeps with a young girl. Unknown to him the girl was under aged and had HIV."

The first consequence he suffers is that of loss of fellowship with God; because God will not tolerate sin, He cuts His fellowship with this brother.
No genuine Believer will like to be in such a situation, because it is a painful place to be if you once enjoyed fellowship with God. A true Believer will feel the pain just like Jesus felt on the cross when the Father forsook Him!
What follows next is the pain of conviction; because he has the Spirit of God in him, the Holy Spirit convicts the brother.

Psalms 51:17 (NIV) says:
"My sacrifice, O God, is a broken spirit; a broken and contrite heart you, God, will not despise."

To be **broken** naturally implies that there will be pain. Therefore, this **broken** brother seeks forgiveness and God forgives him!
However, the day he committed the sin, he sowed different seeds to his flesh and the following happened:

- He sinned against God
- He became unfaithful to his wife
- He contracted STD (AIDS)
- He violated an under aged
- He got her pregnant

So, let us step back for a minute and consider some important points.

The easiest of all to step out of among the five outcomes listed above is the sin against God. Thank God for the blood of Jesus that makes that so very easy!
The Bible says He is faithful and just to forgive us and cleanse us from our unrighteousness if we confess our sins (1 John 1:9)

Afterwards he will need to handle the consequences of the other things this act set in motion. Like, God has forgiven him but now he needs to forgive himself and then he needs his wife to forgive him too. And you know how we humans are with forgiving others. Jesus knew this weakness in us; so, He added it to the Lord's Prayer

Moreover, while going through all that he will have to live with the whispers of friends, family, neighbors, colleagues and church members.

He will still have to face the discipline from the church, and he will have to deal with the sickness he contracted too. No doubt, God can heal him of AIDS even without him asking but he did contract the disease. Then he may be taken to court for violating an under aged, and yes God can deliver him from the court case too! What about the consequences of having a child out of adultery?

My point is this: when we suffer the consequences of our actions, we should know that it is *not God punishing us!* If we sow a lifestyle that is in direct disobedience to God's revealed Word, we ultimately reap disaster.

The consequences of sin may not come immediately but they will come eventually. And when they do, there will be no excuses, no rationalization, no accommodation. *God does not compromise with consequences.*

So, what is the place of grace in all these?
To understand the place of grace in dealing with sin, it is important to combine three verses of scripture

Romans 5:20 (TLB)
*"The Ten Commandments were given so that all could see the extent of their failure to obey God's laws. **But the more we see our sinfulness, the more we see God's abounding grace forgiving us.**" Emphasis mine.*

Roman 6:15 (TLB)
"Does this mean that now we can go ahead and sin and not worry about it? (For our salvation does not depend on keeping the law but on receiving God's grace!) Of course not!" Emphasis mine.

1 Corinthians 10:13(KJV):
"There hath no temptation taken you but such as is common to man: but God is faithful, who will not suffer you to be tempted above that ye are able; but will with the temptation also make a way to escape, that ye may be able to bear it." Emphasis mine

Now let us tie these three scriptures together.
As people sinned more and more, inventing new ways to sin against God, He made His grace sufficient for the forgiveness of sin. (Romans 5:20).
He however does not relish the fact that we take that grace for granted and continue in sin (Roman 6:15); because as a matter of fact, 1 Corinthians 10:13, He personally *"supervises"* the temptation each of us face, ensuring that *we will not* face temptations that will overwhelm us. And so, He makes a way of escape for us so that we can overcome it!

It will be wrong to think that the sole purpose of grace is to cover sin! *God hates sin and He wants us to hate it*

too. That is why when sin comes; the grace to hate, detest and abhor sin comes in increasing measure!

From the above verses of scriptures, we can deduce that when sin abounds God first makes the grace of escape available and when we fail to appropriate that grace then the grace for forgiveness and restoration is offered. One of the ways of escape God has provided for us is abstinence.

1 Thessalonians 5:22 (AMP) tells us to
"Abstain from every form of evil [withdraw and keep away from it]."

Abstinence is the practice of restraining oneself from indulging in sin. We are admonished in this scripture not to linger or hang around any appearance of evil.

James 1:14-15 (NLT) says:
"Temptation comes from our own desires, which entice us and drag us away. These desires give birth to sinful actions. And when sin is allowed to grow, it gives birth to death."

Do not give in to your fleshly desires. It is only when you "entertain" evil or the likeness of it that sin can get hold of you!

I admonish you not to continue to be misguided by those who engage in sin in the name of grace. The author of such teaching is the father of all lies and liars himself. He tells you that grace is available for you to sin, but the Bible forbids us continuing in sin for grace to abound.

*The grace available to us is for **when we do sin, but not to live in sin.***

It is by faith through the grace of God we receive forgiveness of sin when we confess but as *faith without works is dead* so is *repentance without forsaking*. The decision to forsake is one you will need to make yourself.

Proverbs 28:13 (NKJV) says:
" He who covers his sins will not prosper,
But whoever confesses and forsakes them will have mercy."

Grace is tremendously powerful! The Message version of Romans 5:20 says

"... When it's sin versus grace, grace wins hands down."

That is how powerful grace is over sin! It can save the deadliest of sinners and erase their pasts. However, grace will not ask for repentance on your behalf neither will it make the decision for you to forsake your sin.

Simply because God has given us a free will to make such decisions.

In conclusion, know this truth: the ***ultimate grace*** God makes available to us against sin is to be able to detest it and see the way of escape He has provided for us! So why not look out for that way of escape instead and enjoy a continuous unbroken relationship with the Father?

10

The Fear Factor

WE WERE NOT BORN WITH the knowledge of fear; but learn to fear from our parents, siblings, and others around us as we grow up. We also get to learn to fear from other first-hand experiences. We see this unawareness of fear in little children; they can crawl onto the road, put their hands in naked flames, touch hot objects, etc. because they have not had the opportunity to learn the dangers around them yet.

However, many of the things we are afraid of are dangers we have never experienced first-hand! Fear is triggered by two major elements: *real danger* (triggered by actual frightening events) and *"fake" danger* (triggered by our minds!)

The fear triggered by real danger (physical fear) is what science refers to as "fight or flight" mode. When we experience this fear, our adrenal glands release adrenaline into the blood stream, which causes an increase in blood and oxygen flow to our muscles so we can run faster for instance, or act quickly generally.

It also restricts blood flow to other areas of our bodies such as our stomach (that is why hunger is usually the last thing on our minds when we are in danger) Acts 27:33 (MSG)

"With dawn about to break, Paul called everyone together and proposed breakfast: **"This is the fourteenth day we've gone without food. None of us has felt like eating!** *But I urge you to eat something now." Emphasis mine*

This fear also dilates our pupils so we can see better. In this "fight or flight" mode, our senses and reflexes become heightened and it is easy for us to escape real and physical danger. That is all good!

Proverbs 22:3 (NLT) says:
"A prudent person foresees danger and takes precautions. The simpleton **(the naive, the inexperienced)** *goes blindly on and suffers the consequences." Emphasis mine.*

However, the fear triggered by our minds (non-physical) tend to "artificially" force the "fight or flight" mode for self-induced or devil-induced fear!
These fears like stage fright for instance; is all in the mind. The fear of failure, the fear of being hurt, the fear of judgment, the fear of death, etc.
The devil uses the fears he injected into the minds of people to control, manipulate and limit them! Here is the way The Message verse puts 1 John 4:18b

". . . **Since fear is crippling**, *a fearful life—fear of death, fear of judgment—* "*Emphasis mine*

He also uses it as a channel of affliction - both physical and mental!
Proverbs 12:25 (NKJV) says:

*"**Anxiety in the heart of man causes depression**, but a good word makes it glad." Emphasis mine*

Just imagine all the biological and chemical reactions that take place when we face real danger happening in our bodies every time we experience self-induced or devil-induced fear!
Activating the "fight or flight" mode for such fears is detrimental as we end up victims of thoughts because when your thoughts, feelings and decisions are driven by fear, you become a slave of fear.

At this point, fear has become "distorted" and "perverted" and has become a form of oppression that has held many people in bondage causing physical and mental illness. In addition, because the things our minds focus on are the things we tend to attract to our lives, we inadvertently attract the things we fear into our lives.

Job said in Job 3:25 (NIV)
"What I feared has come upon me; what I dreaded has happened to me."

However, the Bible in 2 Timothy 1:7 (KJV) says:

Chapter Ten: The Fear Factor

"For God hath not given us the spirit of fear; but of power, and of love, and of a sound mind."

The devil never wants us to dwell on such scriptures because they set us free from the bondage of fear! He instead wants us to focus on the fear just like the other ten spies in Numbers 13:33, that the devil used fear to distort their reasoning. They were so afraid that they saw themselves as grasshoppers. How in the world did they know how the giants perceived them?

*". . . and we were in our own sight as grasshoppers, **and so we were in their sight.**" Emphasis mine*

Although the Bible says that we should not be afraid so very many times, sometimes we still get scared! There are, however, many ways to deal with fear. Especially the one injected into our minds by the enemy or ourselves; let us look at a few of them.

- *Love*

The first is by love. 1 John 4:18 says:
". . . Well-formed love banishes fear. . ."
Important to notice here that it is not just *"ordinary"* love but *"well-formed"* love. The KJV calls it *"perfect love"*.

Truth is you are never afraid of someone you love or someone who loves you. That is why love is one sure way to counter and banish fear!

1 Cor.13:8a also says:

"Love never fails."

Love is stronger than and conquers all; and that includes fear!

- **Trust in God**

The second way to deal with fear is to run to the Lord and put your trust in Him in prayers. David, in Psalm 56:3-4 (MSG) said:

"When I get really afraid I come to you in trust. *I'm proud to praise God; **fearless now**, I trust in God. What can mere mortals do?" Emphasis mine*

What we do with the fear is what matters; here we see David turning to the Lord and so must we!

- *Renew Your Mind*

The third way to deal with fear, seeing it has been "injected" into our minds, is by renewing our minds!

A mind injected with fear is akin to a web browser that has its browsing data filled up with cached data, cookies and saved website data as well as browsing history. The recommendation is that these data is purged out by clearing the data thereby refreshing and renewing the browsing data.

In the same vein, the mind must be renewed, refreshed, re-constructed and re-calibrated. Romans 12:2 (KJV) says:

*"And be not conformed to this world: but be ye transformed by the **renewing of your mind**, that ye may prove what is that good, and acceptable, and perfect, will of God." Emphasis mine*

- *Meditate on the Word of God*

Closely related to the third is the fourth; which is meditating on the Word of God; focusing on scriptures that encourage us not to fear. The Bible tells us – many times – not to be afraid. Here are a few of them:

"So do not fear, for I am with you; do not be dismayed, for I am your God. I will strengthen you and help you; I will uphold you with my righteous right hand." ~ Isaiah 41:10 (NIV)

"Do not be anxious about anything, but in every situation, by prayer and petition, with thanksgiving, present your requests to God. And the peace of God, which transcends all understanding, will guard your hearts and your minds in Christ Jesus." ~ Philippians 4:6-7 (NIV)

"But now, this is what the Lord says…Fear not, for I have redeemed you; I have summoned you by name; you are mine." ~ Isaiah 43:1 (NIV)

"Have I not commanded you? Be strong and courageous. Do not be terrified; do not be discouraged, for the Lord your God will be with you wherever you go." ~ Joshua 1:9 (NIV)

"Say to those with fearful hearts, "Be strong, and do not fear, for your God is coming to destroy your enemies. He is coming to save you" ~ Isaiah 35:4 (NLT)

The devil uses fear injected into people's minds as a control mechanism; but God does not want us to be afraid of anything; that is why what He's given us is the Spirit of power, and of love, and of a sound mind!

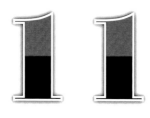

The Health Angle

OUR THOUGHT LIFE PLAYS a major role in determining the state of our health. Many of the things the Bible warns us against is predominantly for our own good. Let us consider two of the many. Two unhealthy emotions that originate from the heart. Anxiety and Anger.

ANXIETY

First, let us look at anxiety.

Anxiety is defined as a feeling of worry, nervousness, or unease about something with an uncertain outcome. It is a feeling that usually co-occurs with fear; and although their symptoms mostly overlap, they are not the same!

It is human nature to feel anxious when facing a challenging situation; we face them daily, a job interview, a tough exam, when faced with making an important decision, etc.

When we become anxious, our bodies respond by releasing a flood of chemicals and hormones like adrenaline into our systems. This is not on its own a bad thing; because these secretions increase our pulses and breathing rate so our brains can get more oxygen and are able to respond appropriately to an intense situation. Afterwards, our bodies return to normal functioning when the stress passes.

That is how God created the body to deal with its environment.

Chapter Eleven: The Health Angle

The problem however arises when one is repeatedly anxious and stressed, or if it lasts for prolonged periods and the body never gets the signal to return to normal functioning. This can weaken the immune system, leaving you more vulnerable to other ailments like loss of appetite, muscle tension, headaches, insomnia, etc.

Whenever there are issues bogging our minds that we have failed to let go to the One who can handle them, we lose our peace, our joy and our sleep. Then our health begins to decline even though the Lord promised us perfect and constant peace if we would just trust in Him!

Isaiah 26:3 (AMP) says:
*"You will keep in perfect and constant peace the one whose **mind** is steadfast [that is, committed and focused on You —in **both inclination and character**], Because he trusts and takes refuge in You [with hope and confident expectation]." Emphasis mine*

It is very important we pay close attention to how we react when faced with anxiety; because it is another mind-injected emotion, the enemy capitalizes on in his scheme to manipulate people.

These mind-injected and enemy-influenced emotions manifest as feelings of terror that come suddenly without warning, breakout of sweat, chest pain,

115

palpitations, etc. sometimes, it is an overwhelming worry and self-consciousness or specific phobias; intense fears of a specific item or situations, such as heights, spiders, swimming or flying.

Many of those plagued by these mind injected and enemy influenced emotions have come to accept it; claiming that is who they are! That is not true; it is yet another lie of the devil and if allowed to persist without correction can lead to disorders that can harm our bodies, our minds and our souls.

That is why the Bible in several scriptures warns against worry and anxiety.

First, by Jesus in Matt. 6: 25-34 (TLB)

*"So my counsel is: **Don't worry about things**—food, drink, and clothes. For you already have life and a body—and they are far more important than what to eat and wear. Look at the birds! They don't worry about what to eat—they don't need to sow or reap or store up food—for your heavenly Father feeds them. And you are far more valuable to him than they are. **Will all your worries add a single moment to your life?** "And why worry about your clothes? Look at the field lilies! They don't worry about theirs. Yet King Solomon in all his glory was not clothed as beautifully as they. And if God cares so wonderfully for flowers that are here today and gone tomorrow, won't he more surely care for you, O men of little faith? "**So don't worry at all** about having enough food and*

clothing. Why be like the heathen? For they take pride in all these things and are deeply concerned about them. But your heavenly Father already knows perfectly well that you need them, and he will give them to you if you give him first place in your life and live as he wants you to.
*"**So don't be anxious about tomorrow.** God will take care of your tomorrow too. Live one day at a time." Emphasis mine*

And then in Luke 12:25-26 (NIV)
"Who of you by worrying can add a single hour to your life?
***Since you cannot do this very little thing, why do you worry about the rest?"** Emphasis mine*

Then Paul the Apostle also admonished in Philippians 4:6-7 (NIV):
*"**Do not be anxious about anything,** but in every situation, by prayer and petition, with thanksgiving, present your requests to God. And the peace of God, which transcends all understanding, will guard your hearts and your minds in Christ Jesus." Emphasis mine*

Let us consider a few reasons why we should be wary of anxiety.

Anxiety is a joy stealer and bad for our health! But a cheerful disposition - joy and laughter is good for our health. The Bible says that gloom and doom; negative

emotions such as anger and frustration can leave us bone-tired or sick.
Proverbs 17:22 (MSG) says

"A cheerful disposition is good for your health; gloom and doom leave you bone-tired"

The joy of a Believer is a strong weapon of victory. That is why the enemy attacks it with anxiety.
Nehemiah 8:10 (KJV) says:
*"Then he said unto them, go your way, eat the fat, and drink the sweet, and send portions unto them for whom nothing is prepared: for this day is holy unto our LORD: neither be ye sorry; **for the joy of the LORD is your strength.**" Emphasis mine*

Anxiety is an energy drainer – it leaves you exhausted! Bone-tired as Proverbs 17:22 (MSG) puts it.
Most of the things we worry and fret about are things beyond our control.
Thousands of researches carried out tell us about the benefits of positive thinking and the disadvantages of negative thinking; and how they affect our health. These researches boil down to what the Bible teaches us! Thousands of years ago, the book of Proverbs in chapter 17 and verse 22 said:

Chapter Eleven: The Health Angle

"A merry heart does good, like medicine, but a broken spirit dries the bones."

ANGER

The second ill we will consider among those the Bible warns us against is anger. Anger they say, is just one letter short of danger! I came across this anonymous quote a couple of years ago and I would like to share it here.

"Anger is the punishment we give ourselves for other people's mistakes"

It is funny but the absolute truth!

Anger is an emotion that emanates from the heart. It is human to be angry; but when it is uncontrolled, that is when it becomes dangerous. The Bible says in Ephesians 4:26 (TLB)

*"**If you are angry**, don't sin **by nursing your grudge. Don't let the sun go down with you still angry**—get over it quickly;" Emphasis mine*

Anger exposes you to the whims of the devil. When God did not accept Cain's offering, he became angry. Genesis 4:4b-5 says:

*"And the Lord accepted Abel's offering, but not Cain's. **This made Cain both dejected and very angry, and his face grew dark with fury.** Emphasis mine*

Cain could not let go of his anger and so, the devil poised
to capitalize on it and God warned him about this plan.
Here is what God said to him in verse 7

"But if you refuse to obey, watch out. **Sin is waiting to
attack you, longing to destroy you.** *But you can conquer
it!" Emphasis mine*

An interesting concept is that there are some of us who
do not want to believe the consequences the Bible warns
us against unless we have scientific proof! Truth is, years
before scientists discovered many of these findings of
theirs, the Bible has sounded the note of warning.
Nevertheless, it is good that most of these findings today
concur with the teachings of the Bible. Without an iota
of doubt, *the spiritual controls the physical as well as
the scientific!* Science simply explains to us how it
happens! So, let us look at what science offers in this
matter.

Scientists have discovered that angry outbursts can
cause an outpouring of stress hormones like adrenaline,
which makes the heart to beat faster and causes blood
pressure to rise and the release of other dangerous
biological and chemical secretions into the body.

Anger puts your heart at great risk; a study found that
there was a three times higher risk of having a stroke

from a blood clot to the brain or bleeding within the brain during the two hours after an angry outburst.

Anger is a powerful emotion. If not dealt with appropriately, may have destructive results for you and those closest to you. Uncontrolled anger can lead to arguments, physical fights, physical abuse, assault and self-harm.

Like Anxiety, anger triggers the body's "fight or flight" response. The adrenal glands flood the body with stress hormones, such as adrenaline and cortisol. The brain shunts blood away from the gut and towards the muscles, in preparation for physical exertion. Heart rate, blood pressure and respiration increase, the body temperature rises, the skin perspires, and the mind becomes sharp and focused. Although these activities of the body themselves are not harmful, it is the constant flooding of stress chemicals and associated metabolic changes that go with recurrent unmanaged anger that eventually cause harm to many different systems of the body.

Some of the short and long-term health problems linked to unmanaged anger include:
- Headaches
- Digestion Problems (such as abdominal pain)
- Insomnia

- Increased Anxiety
- Depression
- High Blood Pressure
- Skin Problems (such as eczema)
- Heart Attack
- Stroke.

So, guard your heart and your mind against these emotions because the consequences of failing to do this are dire. That is why the Bible warns us plainly in Psalm 37:8 (TLB). Where it says:

*"**Stop your anger!** Turn off your wrath. **Don't fret and worry**—it only leads to harm." Emphasis mine*

12

Activate the Peace of Christ

YOU ALREADY HAVE THE PEACE of God! It may not be all around you; but it is within you! Jesus, in John 14:27 (AMP) said:

"Peace I leave with you; My [perfect] peace I give to you; not as the world gives do I give to you. Do not let your heart be troubled, nor let it be afraid. [Let My perfect peace calm you in every circumstance and give you courage and strength for every challenge.] Emphasis mine

Do you have the Spirit of God in you? If your answer is yes, then see what Galatians 5:22 (NLT) says:

*"But the Holy Spirit produces this kind of fruit in our lives: love, joy, **peace,** patience, kindness, goodness, faithfulness," Emphasis mine*

Well, there you go! You have it! Period! The question however is this: *"Is peace activated and ruling your life?"*

Colossians 3:15a (NIV) says,
*"Let **(allow)** the peace of Christ **rule in your hearts,"** Emphasis mine*

The peace of Christ brings order where there is chaos in every heart that allows it to be in control. It is the major guard and protector of our hearts and minds; but it needs to be activated and ruling in our lives before we can enjoy these benefits. Philippians 4:6-7 (AMP) says:

*"Do not be anxious or worried about anything, but in everything [every circumstance and situation] by prayer and petition with thanksgiving, continue to make your [specific] requests known to God. **And the peace of God [that peace which reassures the heart, that peace] which transcends all understanding, [that peace which] stands guard over your hearts and your minds in Christ Jesus** [is yours]."* Emphasis mine

From this passage of scripture, we learn that it is this peace:

- **That reassures the heart** *when all around you there is chaos.*
- **That rises above all understanding** *when there is confusion all around.*
- **That stands guard over your hearts and your minds** *in Christ Jesus.*

To activate something is to **make it active or operative**. It implies that a thing has certain potentials lying dormant that needs turning on to get them operational. Jesus has already given us peace; all we need do now is to activate it.

Let us consider six ways to activate the peace within us so it can rule in our hearts:

1. Decide
This is the first step of three in Philippians 4:6-7 (AMP) that will help unlock the peace of God. It says,

*"**Do not be anxious or worried about anything**, but in everything [every circumstance and situation] by prayer and petition with thanksgiving, continue to make your [specific] requests known to God. And the peace of God [that peace which reassures the heart, that peace] which transcends all understanding, [that peace which] stands guard over your hearts and your minds in Christ Jesus [is yours]." Emphasis mine*

Decide not to be anxious about anything!
Easier said than done right?
It becomes *"easier done"* too when we come to realize that our worrying gets nothing done. Hear Jesus' own words in Luke 12:25-26 (NIV)

"Who of you by worrying can add a single hour to your life? Since you cannot do this very little thing, why do you worry about the rest?"

Will you not agree then; and does it not therefore make absolute sense that continuing to worry is pointless; seeing you achieve nothing by it?

2. *Pray*

The second step is prayers; commit whatever the situation is to the Almighty God **specifically** and **continually** in prayers. Philippians 4:6-7 (AMP) says,

*"Do not be anxious or worried about anything, but in everything [every circumstance and situation] **by prayer and petition** with thanksgiving, **continue to make your [specific] requests** known to God. And the peace of God [that peace which reassures the heart, that peace] which transcends all understanding, [that peace which] stands guard over your hearts and your minds in Christ Jesus [is yours]." Emphasis mine*

3. *Give Thanks*

The third of the three steps is another ***"easier said than done"*** situation isn't it?

1 Thessalonians 5:18 (AMP) says:

*"**Thank (God) in everything** (no matter what the circumstances may be, be thankful and give thanks), for this is the will of God for you (who are) in Christ Jesus (the Revealer and Mediator of that will)." Emphasis mine*

Giving thanks and praise to God; *no matter what the circumstances may be is difficult but possible;* it is easy when we form the habit of thanksgiving long before we face difficult circumstances.

Our mantle scripture Philippians 4:6-7 (AMP) says,

*"Do not be anxious or worried about anything, but in everything [every circumstance and situation] by prayer and petition **with thanksgiving**, continue to make your [specific] requests known to God. And the peace of God [that peace which reassures the heart, that peace] which transcends all understanding, [that peace which] stands guard over your hearts and your minds in Christ Jesus [is yours]." Emphasis mine*

4. Believe

The fourth we will consider is to rid ourselves of doubt and unbelief and believe! It is as we believe in God; we become full of His peace. Romans 15:13 (TLB) says:

*"So I pray for you Gentiles that God who gives you hope will keep you happy and **full of peace as you believe in him**. I pray that God will help you overflow with hope in him through the Holy Spirit's power within you." Emphasis mine*

5. Trust in the Lord

Isaiah 26:3 (KJV) says:

*"**Thou wilt keep him in perfect peace**, whose mind is stayed on thee: **because he trusteth in thee**." Emphasis mine*

So, decide to trust God and not lose sleep at night due to worry because God keeps a constant vigil. The Bible says in Psalm 121:4 (KJV):

"Behold, he that keepeth Israel shall neither slumber nor sleep."

Will you not also agree that it is therefore unnecessary for you to lose sleep? It makes no sense for two people to lose sleep over one issue!

6. *Speak It!*

We have the power to issue decrees and cause the elements to obey us! In Mark 11: 23 (NIV); after the cursing and withering of the fig tree, Jesus said to Peter:

"Truly I tell you, if anyone says to this mountain, 'Go, throw yourself into the sea,' and does not doubt in their heart but believes that what they say will happen, it will be done for them.

In addition, when the disciples became sore afraid that they would perish in the sea, Jesus spoke to the raging sea. Mark 4: 39 (NKJV):

"Then He arose and rebuked the wind, and said to the sea, ***"Peace, be still!"*** *And the wind ceased and there was a great calm."* *Emphasis mine*

The ultimate guardian of the heart and mind is the peace of Christ! You already have it! Activate it and let it rule in your heart!

"And ***the peace of God*** *[that peace which reassures the heart, that peace] which transcends all understanding, [that peace which]* ***stands guard over your hearts and your minds in Christ Jesus [is yours]."*** *Philippians 4:7 (AMP) Emphasis mine*

Put on The Full Armour

T HERE IS AN ONGOING battle in the spiritual realm where unseen forces are contending to take control of the minds of people whether you believe it or not! For an individual to be ignorant, sceptical or nonchalant about this truth places them in a precarious position and exposes them as cheap prey to the prowling predator, the devil.

It is important, especially for the Believer, to be aware that this war is not against flesh and blood but against the spiritual forces of wickedness and darkness. No one walks into a battle unprepared; to do this or arrive unequipped is as precarious as the case of one who is ignorant.

The Bible in 2 Cor. 10:4-5 tells us that the weapons of this warfare we are engaged in are not carnal (physical) but are mighty for pulling down strongholds. Paul was in effect saying, *"you don't bring a knife to a gun fight"*. We must therefore be adequately equipped for this battle.

In this chapter, we shall be exploring the six components of the Believer's armour we need to put on and take up for the protection of our hearts and minds. In Ephesians 6: 10-18 the Apostle Paul introduces us to the Believer's Armour:

"In conclusion, be strong in the Lord [draw your strength from Him and be empowered through your union with Him] and in the power of His [boundless] might. Put on the full armour of God [for His precepts are like the splendid armour of a heavily armed soldier], so that you may be able to [successfully] stand up against all the schemes and the strategies and the deceits of the devil. For our struggle is not against flesh and blood [contending only with physical opponents], but against the rulers, against the powers, against the world forces of this [present] darkness, against the spiritual forces of wickedness in the heavenly (supernatural) places. Therefore, put on the complete armour of God, so that you will be able to [successfully] resist and stand your ground in the evil day [of danger], and having done everything [that the crisis demands], to stand firm [in your place, fully prepared, immovable, victorious]. So stand firm and hold your ground, having tightened the **wide band of truth** *(personal integrity, moral courage) around your waist and having put on* **the breastplate of righteousness (an upright heart),** *and having strapped on your feet* **the gospel of peace in preparation** *[to face the enemy with firm-footed stability and the readiness produced by the good news]. Above all, lift up the [protective]* **shield of faith** *with which you can extinguish all the flaming arrows of the evil one. And take* **the helmet of salvation**, *and* **the sword of the Spirit**, *which is the Word of God. With all prayer and petition pray [with specific requests] at all times [on every occasion and in every season] in the Spirit, and with this in*

view, stay alert with all perseverance and petition [interceding in prayer] for all God's people." (AMP) Emphasis mine

Here are the things we must do.

1. Wear Truth as a Belt

We live in a darkened, deceptive world. The devil is constantly deceiving the whole world with his lies. He has mastered the art of slightly skewing the truth in the name of "white lies", etc. and that nothing like absolute truth exists. But in today's world drifting without absolutes, we can use these words of Jesus Christ in John 14:6 and John 17:17 as the absolute truth!

"Jesus saith unto him, **I am the way, the truth, and the life***: no man cometh unto the Father, but by me." John 14:6(KJV) Emphasis mine*

"Sanctify them by Your truth. **Your word is truth***". John 17:17(KJV) Emphasis mine.*

Believers must be totally committed to truth, who God is, what God has said and what God has done. When as Believers we apply the truth in our lives and allow it to be our guide, we are spiritually protected from Satan's attacks. It does not prevent these attacks; but it prevents us from being bound by them!

John 8:32 (KJV) says:

"And ye shall know the truth, and the truth shall make you free."

We must faithfully hold the truth of God's word, **but it is also necessary for the truth to hold us.** Unless we are motivated and directed by truth (personal integrity, moral courage), we will be defeated by the enemy. If we permit any deception to enter our lives, we have weakened our position and cannot fight the battle victoriously.

2. Wear Righteousness as a Breastplate

Zechariah 3:1 tells us of the story of Joshua the high priest who was under accusation by the devil.

*"Then the angel showed me Jeshua the high priest standing before the angel of the LORD. The Accuser, Satan, was there at the angel's right hand, **making accusations against Jeshua."** (NLT)* Emphasis mine.

The devil is in the constant business of mudslinging and accusing Believers. Wearing righteousness as a breastplate protects our hearts from condemnation when he comes against us to distort the truth of our right standing with God; trying to derail us from the path of holiness. This "Righteousness" worn is in two dimensions for a Christian.

- ***Righteousness by faith***

This is the righteousness of Christ implanted in us at salvation, it fortifies the heart against the attacks of Satan. Rom.3:21-22 (NKJV)

"But now the righteousness of God apart from the law is revealed, being witnessed by the Law and the Prophets, even the righteousness of God, through faith in Jesus Christ, to all and on all who believe. For there is no difference"

- ***Righteousness by lifestyle/practice***

The second dimension of righteousness is by practice. It is living a godly life by the tenets of God's Word; having an upright heart, being filled with the Holy Spirit; working and living faithfully for the Lord and living a righteous life. Eph.4:21-24 (KJV) says:

"if indeed you have heard Him and have been taught by Him, as the truth is in Jesus: that you put off, concerning your former conduct, the old man which grows corrupt according to the deceitful lusts, and be renewed in the spirit of your mind, and that you put on the new man which was created according to God, in true righteousness and holiness."

Ps.106:3 (NKJV) also talks about this second dimension of righteousness.
"Blessed are those who keep justice, and he who does righteousness at all times!"

3. Wear Readiness of the Gospel of Peace as Shoes

Having on the shoes of readiness of the Gospel of peace implies that we should be ready to move with the Gospel! The word readiness implies constant vigilance. Like the wise virgins (Matthew 25:1-13). It implies that one is prepared for battle. When we are ready/prepared with the Gospel of peace, we live with the understanding that we are continually under attack from Satan and therefore never let our guards down. 1 Peter 5:8 (NIV) says:

"Be alert and of sober mind. Your enemy the devil prowls around like a roaring lion looking for someone to devour.

We also cannot live a chaotic life and be able to offer peace to others. So, it is important that we have
Peace with God (Romans 5:1).
"Therefore, since we have been justified through faith, we have peace with God through our Lord Jesus Christ," (NIV)
Peace within (Psalm 4:8).
"In peace, I will lie down and sleep, for you alone, Lord, make me dwell in safety." (NIV)
Peace with others (Romans 12:18).
"If it be possible, as much as lieth in you, live peaceably with all men" (KJV)

The devil offers lots of distractions, encourages procrastination and promotes nonchalance; but we are able to overcome these by having our feet fitted with the

readiness that comes from the gospel of peace because being prepared to move with the Gospel changes the atmosphere to that of urgency!

It also means that we have confidence of our position in Christ; *a balanced life on solid footing.* Not like those who are tossed to and fro by every wind of doctrine. Instead, we stand our ground and confidently face the enemy with firm-footed stability.

4. Lift up Faith as a Shield

The purpose of taking up the shield of faith is so that we can quench the fiery darts of the enemy providing security and protection against the assaults of the Devil.

The shield is the first line of defence; it guards, deflects and can also incapacitate the enemy.

A shield, whether it be physical or spiritual, can only be effective when it is lifted. Hence Paul's admonishment to *lift it up.*

Lifting up faith as a shield is vital to guarding our hearts and mind for many reasons. Let us look at three of them.

We have been justified by faith. Romans 5:1-2 (NKJV) says:

"Therefore, having been justified by faith, we have peace with God through our Lord Jesus Christ, through whom also we have access by faith into this grace in which we stand, and rejoice in hope of the glory of God". Emphasis mine

When the enemy throws the fiery dart of temptation at our minds; we deflect the dart by lifting up our faith as a shield because:

We overcome the devil by faith 1 John 5:4 (KJV) says:
"For whatever is born of God overcomes the world. ***And this is the victory that has overcome the world—our faith"*** *Emphasis mine*

The ultimate reason for the devil's assault against us is to cause us to rebel against God like when iniquity was found in him (Isaiah 14:13-14). So, when he throws the fiery dart of deceit at us so we can rebel against God like in the Garden of Eden; we lift up our faith as a shield to deflect it because:

Faith makes it possible for us to please God Hebrews 11:6a (NIV)
*"****And without faith it is impossible to please God****, because anyone who comes to him must believe that he exists and that he rewards those who earnestly seek him."* *Emphasis mine*

5. Wear the Hope of Salvation as a Helmet

In Chapter Two we looked at a few of the devil's tricks. One of them being "You are Helpless and Hopeless". With this trick, he uses people and situations to instil the belief in the minds of his victims. And once he's able to get into their minds this way he has them trapped, and he takes over the reins of their minds.

The helmet of the hope of salvation is the great hope of our **final salvation.** It protects us against this trick by giving us the confidence and assurance that we will be victorious in the end. 1 Thessalonians 5:8-9 (NKJV) says:

*"But let us who are of the day be sober, putting on the breastplate of faith and love, and **as a helmet the hope of salvation.** For God did not appoint us to wrath, but to obtain salvation through our Lord Jesus Christ."*

Matthew 10:22 (NKJV) says:
*"And you will be hated by all for My name's sake. **But he who endures to the end will be saved".***

1 Peter 1:4-5 (NLT) also says:
"and we have a priceless inheritance—an inheritance that is kept in heaven for you, pure and undefiled, beyond the reach of change and decay. And through your faith, God is protecting you by his power until you receive this salvation, which is ready to be revealed on the last day for all to see."

We need to keep this hope of the glorious future with our Lord in view because if we lose hope in the future promise of salvation or lose sight of the eternal, the enemy can use this as a legal ground to inject discouragement and despair into our hearts and minds.

6. Take up the Word of God as a Sword
The Sword of the Spirit is the Word of God.

The Sword Is Our Weapon of Offence
The best defence they say, is a good offense. The general idea behind this adage is that proactivity *(a strong offensive action)* instead of a passive attitude will preoccupy the opposition and ultimately hinder their ability to mount an opposing counterattack, leading to a strategic advantage. We need to take up the Sword of the Spirit because if we sit back and wait for the enemy's attack, we could someday become discouraged and give in. But if we are on the offensive, we put the enemy on the back foot. Hebrews 4:12 (NKJV) says:

"For the word of God is living and powerful, and sharper than any two-edged sword, piercing even to the division of soul and spirit, and of joints and marrow, and is a discerner of the thoughts and intents of the heart."

The all-powerful Sword of the Living God is able to cut through every defence our enemy can raise—down to the very division of bone and marrow.

The Sword Is Also for Defence
The Word of God valuable in defending against spiritual attack. When Jesus Christ Himself was tempted by Satan in Matthew 4, He took up the Word of God as His defence.

"And when the tempter came to him, he said, if thou be the Son of God, command that these stones be made bread." (verse 3) (KJV).

"But he answered and said, it is written, Man shall not live by bread alone, but by every word that proceedeth out of the mouth of God.'" (verse 4) (KJV).

Satan's second attempt was twisting the scriptures. He quoted Psalms 91:11-12
"Then the devil took Him up into the holy city, set Him on the pinnacle of the temple, and said to Him, 'If You are the Son of God, throw Yourself down. For it is written: "He shall give the angels charge over you," and, "In their hands they shall bear you up, lest you dash your foot against a stone"'" (verses 5-6). (NKJV)

Here is how Jesus responded
"It is written again, 'You shall not tempt the LORD your God'"

Satan made one final attempt:
"Again, the devil took Him up on an exceedingly high mountain and showed Him all the kingdoms of the world and their glory. And he said to Him, 'All these things I will give You if You will fall down and worship me'" (Matthew 4:8-9). (NKJV)

Again, the final answer in the next verse comes from the scriptures (Deuteronomy 6:13):

"Then Jesus said to him, 'Away with you, Satan! For it is written, "You shall worship the LORD your God, and Him only you shall serve"'" (verse 10) (NKJV).

For each temptation, Jesus made use of the Word (the Sword of the Spirit) to deflect the attacks.

The Word of God in the mouth of a Believer is a potent weapon for both offence and defence; we must take it up to protect our hearts and minds!

Ten Powerhouse Protocols

ALL TRUTH IS PARALLEL; in warfare, warring parties strategically target strongholds, and/or critical infrastructure of their enemies or prevent access to them. They may for instance, destroy a power station or blow up a bridge in an attempt to weaken their adversary.

The ongoing battle in the spiritual realm by the devil and his cohorts is targeted at taking control of the mind of people; because if successful, they will be in control of their powerhouses and the battle is as good as lost for them!

The world today is experiencing an unprecedented level of widespread depravity because of this ongoing battle for the control of the minds of the people. So far, the enemy has succeeded in capturing millions of the unsuspecting and the naïve; those with unguarded and unprotected hearts and minds by offering depravity disguised as "liberation".

When God initially created the mind of man, He checked and saw that it was good! However, after the fall of man, the mind became susceptible to the antics of the enemy and he is still engaged in his mind games until today.

Although the mind became susceptible to the antics of the enemy, it was not completely left devoid of God! The human conscience remained; and it continued to keep us in check, so we do not stray away from who He meant us to be.

God, however, did more than just leave us with a conscience; He redeemed us and consequently our minds by His Son Jesus and gave us the mind of Christ. The enemy does not want to let go of the control he had over our minds, so he daily engages in a battle to win our minds back.

Human nature is to naturally treat things that did not cost us with levity; but we should know that although we got our redemption free, it was not cheap! Jesus paid a great price for it! The responsibility then is on us to preserve and protect our hearts and minds and not treat them like trash by letting trash dwell in it!

1 Peter 1:13 (NLT) says:
*"So **prepare your minds** for action and **exercise self-control**. Put all your hope in the gracious salvation that will come to you when Jesus Christ is revealed to the world." Emphasis mine*

The enemy operates by suggesting thoughts in people's minds. These thoughts if allowed to stay, take a foothold in the mind and they will most definitely become strongholds; and not long after, the devil has control of that mind! You can choose what you think! 1 Peter 1:13 admonishes us to prepare our minds well in advance; to make the decision that we will not engage in the things contrary to the Spirit. The NKJV says:

"Therefore gird up the loins of your mind. . ."

To gird, is to bind, to restrain, to fix or to tighten it ready for battle!

In the previous two chapters, we looked at *activating the peace of God*, which stands guard over our hearts and our minds in Christ Jesus and *putting on the full armour of God* to ward off the fiery darts the enemy fires at our hearts and minds.

In this chapter, we shall be looking at ten additional protocols we can engage in guarding our hearts and minds (our powerhouse).

1. Shut Evil Thoughts Out: Do Not Let Them in!

This is the first protocol we need to employ in protecting our hearts and minds. Actually, the easiest way to deal with evil thoughts is not to let them in, in the first place. Because once they are in, they dart all over the place; and attempting to deal with them is synonymous to chasing a mouse in a gallery with delicate antiques.

In addition, evil thoughts are like muddy shoes leaving stains, smells and filth all over the house. We would normally take muddy shoes off and leave them just outside by the backdoor right? We should treat evil thoughts in the same way.

Ephesians 4:27 (NIV) says:
"And do not give the devil a foothold"

When we entertain thoughts that are not right, we are giving the devil a foothold and in no time, he can make that foothold a stronghold!

So, here is how to handle negative thoughts. Once a negative thought enters your mind, interrupt it and replace it with a positive one. If for instance, your eyes are closed and the evil thought comes, open them; if they are opened, close them! Interrupt them.
However, note that negative thoughts will not just turn around and leave, they will want to return. So, if they do, continue to replace them with positive thoughts for as long as they return! Never give up! If you persist, you will eventually teach your mind to think positively, and to ignore negative thoughts.

Nearly 30 years ago, I moved from Benin City to live in Lagos state in Nigeria and I soon discovered that living in Lagos was very different from living in Benin City. One of the "feats" I got interested in was jumping into moving "Molue" buses.

Sometimes all I needed was to be able to grab unto the pole at the entrance of the bus and get a foot in even if the other parts of my body were afloat outside the bus. All I needed was a foothold! Many times, in a few minutes, people would have moved around, I would have my two feet planted firmly on the bus, and as other passengers got off the bus, I ended up having a seat on the bus!

The devil operates in a similar fashion, all he needs initially is a foothold and before you know it, his two feet are firmly planted, and then he is able to take over! So, shut the door! Keep out the devil!

Before we conclude this first way of protecting our hearts and minds, I will like to draw our attention to another truth. Ephesians 5:15 (KJV) says:
"See then that ye walk circumspectly, not as fools, but as wise"

You and I will agree that we would not struggle to discard a thought if it introduced itself and revealed its manifesto. If it for instance said:

"Hi, my name is "thought", I'm going to subtly get into your head and encourage you to get involved in pornography. While I am at it, I will help you rationalise your involvement. My

ultimate plan, however, is to get you involved in masturbation, fornication, adultery and other forms of perversion. All the while I will prevent you from seeing how I am messing you up and wrecking your life and destroying your destiny and I will make you see nothing wrong with it. And do not bother about what Proverbs 14:12 says about a way that appears to be right; but in the end, it leads to death – that is just being over dramatic! But anyway, one day when you are either at the verge of greatness or just when you have become great, I will expose and disgrace you and bring you down to nothing!" But hey! Do not mind me, I am just an innocent thought – nothing to worry about; carry on!

Alternatively, what about if it introduced itself like this?

*"Hi, my name is "thought", I'm going to subtly get into your head and encourage you to do whatever you like; to live free and try all sorts of substances. Initially, it will be occasional and recreational; **only** when you are hanging out with friends, but the plan will be to get you addicted that you will be ready to do anything to get high. Then you will lose your job, become homeless, and begin to live rough. From there, it is a slippery slope. You will start engaging in anything and everything including armed robbery to feed the addiction. You will also start selling yourself for these drugs and then one day you will overdose and die.*

Hmmm . . . or maybe, you prefer the second option?

When I finally get your head filled with how much you have failed yourself and everyone, I will then convince you to commit suicide. No?
There is a third option though, while high, you will rape and murder someone and get the penalty for it!
But don't let me get in your way, just proceed without caution!
When has merely thinking a thing done anyone any harm?"

Of course, in a flash you and I will discard the thought. However, when these thoughts come, they do not announce their complete manifestos. Instead, they point you to the *"pleasures"* of the here and now. But, Proverbs 14:12 (NIV) says:

"There is a way that appears to be right but in the end, it leads to death."

So, go ahead and discard the thoughts as soon as they rear their ugly heads! You will be better for it!

2. Renew Your Mind – Daily!

The second way of protecting our hearts and minds is its daily renewal with the Word of God; because of the tremendous power of the Word!
Hebrews 4:12 (NKJV) says:

"For the word of God is living and powerful, and sharper than any two-edged sword, piercing even to the division of soul and

spirit, and of joints and marrow, **and is a discerner of the thoughts and intents of the heart.**" *Emphasis mine*

To "renew" simply means to make (something) new, fresh, or strong again to give fresh life or strength to something!

The renewal of the mind can be likened to polishing an artefact, servicing a car, cleaning the house, etc. All these actions are measures that protect our properties from wear, tear, and degeneration. You can only successfully take the reins of your mind by renewing it (giving it life) daily with the Word of God – to think otherwise is dangerous and deceptive! Romans 12:2a (NIV) says:

"Do not conform to the pattern of this world but be transformed by the renewing of your mind."

Renewing the mind must be taken as a daily and continuous project. The process of renewing one's mind involves offloading negative, sinful, and limiting thoughts and replacing them with positive, righteous and unlimited thoughts. It is not only offloading evil or negative thoughts but also replacing them with thoughts that are **good, right** and **true**!

This is important because according to the ancient philosopher Aristotle, ***"Nature abhors a vacuum."***

Aristotle based his conclusion on the observation that nature requires every space to be filled with something, even if that something is colourless, odourless air.

We should not be ignorant of the devices of the devil the Bible advices. So, here is one device we should be aware of:

Luke 11:24 - 26 (NIV) says:

*"When an impure spirit comes out of a person, it goes through arid places seeking rest and does not find it. Then it says, '**I will return to the house I left.**' When it arrives, it finds the house swept clean and put in order. **Then it goes and takes seven other spirits more wicked than itself, and they go in and live there. And the final condition of that person is worse than the first.**" Emphasis mine*

Every time we get rid of evil thoughts from our minds, we likewise get rid of the demon introducing the thoughts. But according to the scripture, it goes through dry places looking for a place to rest and not finding returns even more dogged!

Those who have left their minds idle – become cheap prey. For those who have filled their minds with the Word of God have all sorts of attacks launched against their minds – seeking to wear them out!

These attacks are targeted at making us conform to the pattern of this world, to the desires of our flesh and to the bidding of the enemy. Thus, renewing of our minds with the Word of God is a divine countermeasure that makes our minds and our resolve to guard our hearts with all diligence new, fresh, and strong again; and if there had been a slip, it transforms us back to God's original intention.

Make it a continuous project and daily take the time out to renew your mind!

3. Align Your Thoughts with God's Words.

To align a thing is to put it into correct or appropriate relative position with something else. It also means to come together in agreement or alliance with something or someone.

To align our thoughts with God's words therefore means to bring our thoughts to agree, or in alliance with the Word of God! In Psalms 119:11 (NLT), the Psalmist said:

"I have hidden your word in my heart that I might not sin against you."

The Word of God hidden in our hearts serve as a deterrent to sin. Jeremiah 17:9 (MSG) tells us that

*"**The heart is hopelessly dark and deceitful**, a puzzle that no one can figure out." Emphasis mine*

It is for this reason (the fallen nature of the natural mind) that we sometimes surprise ourselves by the thoughts that stray into our minds. In the NIV version, a rhetorical question was asked of the mind, *"Who can understand it?"* Then in verse 10, God answers:

*"But I, God, **search the heart and examine the mind**. I get to the heart of the human. I get to the root of things. I treat them as they really are, not as they pretend to be." (MSG) Emphasis mine*

Paul also answered the question in Hebrews 4:12 when he said:

*"The Word of God is quick, and powerful, and sharper than any two-edged sword, piercing even to the dividing asunder of soul and spirit, and of the joints and marrow, **and is a discerner of the thoughts and intents of the heart."** (KJV) Emphasis mine.*

Paul's admonishment in Philippians 4:8 (KJV) is for us to take the reins of our minds and guide them through only paths that are *good, **true*** and ***right**!*

 *"Finally, brethren, whatever things are **true**, whatever things are **noble**, whatever things are **just**, whatever things are pure, whatever things are lovely, whatever things are of good report,*

if there is any virtue and if there is anything praiseworthy—meditate on these things." Emphasis mine

If our minds follow "paths" that are **good, true** and **right;** then rest assured, we will be able to think about things that are **pure** and **lovely**, and able to dwell on the **fine, good things in others**. Finally, able to think **about all we can praise God for and be glad about.**

The contrary however, is the case with "paths" that are bad, false and wrong you will be unable to think about things that are pure and lovely, instead you will have impure thoughts of all sorts and start to dwell on the ugliest and worst things in others. Finally, you will be continually ungrateful and unhappy!

So, bring your thoughts into cooperation, agreement and alignment with the Word of God and what it says about you!

4. Acknowledge the Lord!

Acknowledging the Lord implies that you have Him always in view no matter what! In your thoughts, your words and your actions.

The direction the world is heading today is one that fails to acknowledge God for who He is! So, let us be careful not to follow the crowd because the consequences can be dire. In Romans, 1:28 the Bible tells us of what happens to those who fail to acknowledge Him:

*"And even as **they did not like to retain God in their knowledge,** God gave them over to a reprobate **(depraved)** mind, to do those things which are not convenient **(things which are improper and repulsive);"** (KJV) Emphasis mine*

You see, it is not that they were completely ignorant about God; but they just *did not like the idea of retaining God in their knowledge!*

They had some knowledge of God by the light of nature, and yet did not care. That is exactly what we are seeing these days. Because they do not want to retain God in their knowledge, they are trying every method to erase this knowledge of God out of their minds, and from others!

Therefore, God gave them up to doing everything their evil minds could think of – a reprobate mind. A mind that is unprincipled, roguish, bad, wicked, shameless, immoral, degenerate, depraved, corrupt and hardened.

One simple way of acknowledging the Lord in this light as Believers is by not being intimidated or embarrassed mentioning Him in our conversations! Because the goal of the opposition is to erase the knowledge of God out of their minds and from others; and they have not given themselves any boundaries! You are a target too!

They are very comfortable and upfront about their depravity; in fact, they flaunt it! We must also be very comfortable and upfront about our relationship with God and be ready and willing to flaunt it boldly!

A very practical way of acknowledging the Lord for example is when people want to know how you were able to accomplish a task that they did not expect you to have accomplished for instance, you acknowledge the Lord without any reservation.

You start with . . .
"Oh! Thanks! I was able to accomplish it by what we refer to as grace. You know, grace is when God lends someone a helping hand. And I am grateful to God for that"

If they pass a compliment, you say:
"Oh! Thanks for the compliment. You are so kind! You see, I have been tremendously blessed by God. And I am grateful to Him for that"

Always having at the back of your mind that the enemy will not succeed in erasing the knowledge of God from yours or anyone's heart and mind under your watch!

5. Meditate on The Word

This way of protecting the heart and mind has dual benefits! Because meditation on the Word does not only protect the mind from the devil's attack but makes us blessed, prosperous and successful!

To meditate means to *focus* one's thoughts on, reflect on or ponder over. From this definition, we can correctly infer that; to meditate means to focus one's thoughts *on something- not many things,* to reflect *on one matter not all matters* at hand or ponder *over something not everything* the keyword being "focus"

The process of Biblical meditation does not only lead to revelation from God but it also "empties" the mind of the wrong things and "fills" it with what is right, good and true according to God's Word. The Bible in Joshua 1:8 and Psalm 1:2 admonishes us to meditate on the Word day and night (in other words, all of our waking moments; when we have control of our minds). God also told Joshua to ensure the words do not "depart" because that is the only way to prevent replacement by any other words or thoughts.

"This Book of the Law shall not depart from your mouth, but you shall read [and meditate on] it day and night, so that you may be careful to do [everything] in accordance with all that is

written in it; for then you will make your way prosperous, and then you will be successful." Joshua 1:8 (AMP)

"But his delight is in the law of the Lord, and on His law [His precepts and teachings] he [habitually] meditates day and night." Psalm 1:2 (AMP)

It is however, "almost" impossible that the thoughts that come across our minds every waking moment are God's Words or in general, good thoughts. So, it is possible that "unwanted" thoughts could stray into our minds. That these "unwanted" thoughts come is not the issue because we mostly cannot control them coming in. What we do with them is what matters.

So, do not engage with or dwell on wrong thoughts – do not give them the "light" of day! Instead, engage with and dwell on the Word of God. With your mind meditating on the Word day and night, there will be no room for wrong thoughts to take root and dominate your mind! In addition, as a bonus you make your way prosperous and become successful in life!

A simple practical rule is this:

"If you need to dwell on any thought, make sure it is that which is good, true and right!"

6. Avoid Garbage

You must have once heard this popular cliché – Garbage in Garbage Out. Interestingly, it does not apply only to the computer world but our minds too! Even more importantly is that the idea originated from the Bible! In Galatians 6:8 (KJV) the Bible says:

*"Be not deceived; God is not mocked: for whatsoever a man soweth, that shall he also reap. For **he that soweth to his flesh (Garbage in) shall of his flesh reap corruption (Garbage out);** but he that soweth to the Spirit shall of the Spirit reap life everlasting."* Emphasis mine

Romans 8:6 (NIV) also further buttresses the point:

"The mind governed by the flesh is death, but the mind governed by the Spirit is life and peace."

Simply put, do not allow "garbage" into your minds because you will get "garbage" in your life. There is a popular quote attributed to Benjamin Franklin's Poor Richard's Almanack. It says:
"He that lieth down with dogs shall rise up with fleas"

It is also an act of foolishness to allow "garbage" into your mind. Proverbs 15:14 (NLT) says:

*"A wise person is hungry for knowledge, while **the fool feeds on trash**".*

Instead of feeding on "garbage", seek knowledge, seek the Truth! John 8:32 (KJV) says:

*"And you shall **know** the truth and the truth shall make you free."*

If you notice that, during the time of your mind battles, your spirit offers very little resistance to your flesh and it is simply bulldozed away by your flesh dragging you into sin; know that it is because you have failed to *"sow enough to your spirit".* That is why it has therefore become impoverished; and that is why your flesh has so much power over your spirit.

What happens during your mind battles when the devil is invoking your flesh to war against your spirit, the devil uses the garbage as legal ground and trying to resist him becomes futile.

If you cannot say for definite like Jesus that *"the evil one cometh but found nothing of his in me"* then pay attention to what you allow into your mind!
Recall again, what 1 Peter 1:13. (NKJV) says:

*"**Therefore gird up the loins of your mind**, be sober, and rest your hope fully upon the grace that is to be brought to you at the revelation of Jesus Christ;"* Emphasis mine

To gird, is to bind, to restrain, to fix or to tighten. The mind must be tightened and protected to make no room for trash.

7. Keep A Clear Conscience

Our conscience is meant to check and correct us; but when we ignore it *(deliberately violate it)* and continue in error it begins to sear slowly *(it slowly begins to lose the ability to reflect who God intended for us to be)* and we lose our check and head for ruin.

The Bible says in 1 John 3:21 (NLT):

"Dear friends, if our hearts do not condemn us, we have confidence before God"

Paul writing in 1 Timothy 1:19 (NLT) said:

*"Cling to your faith in Christ, and **keep your conscience clear**. For some people have deliberately violated their consciences; as a result, their faith has been shipwrecked."* Emphasis mine

To keep a clear conscience means you are not harbouring anything within that "violates" or "sears" it!

Lying for instance violates our consciences. 1 Timothy 4:2 (KJV) says:
"Speaking lies in hypocrisy; having their conscience seared with a hot iron"

Holding onto offence also violates our consciences
In Acts 24:16 (KJV) Paul said:
"And herein do I exercise myself, to have always a conscience void to offence toward God, and toward men."

To maintain a conscience void of offence three things are necessary.

- *Be Principled:* Live your life guided by Bible based principles. Proverbs 11:4 MSG says:
  *"A thick bankroll is no help when life falls apart, but a **principled life** can stand up to the worst."*

- *Be Impartial:* Maintain an impartial comparison of your conduct with those principles. 1 Timothy 5:21 (NASB) says:
  *"I solemnly charge you in the presence of God and of Christ Jesus and of His chosen angels, to **maintain these principles without bias, doing nothing in a spirit of partiality**." Emphasis mine*

- *Be Sincere:* Be sincere in your assessment; ensure you are not deceiving yourself.
  Psalm 101:2b (KJV) says:

*"I will walk **within my house** with a perfect heart."*
Emphasis mine

8. Set Your Mind on Things Above
Set your mind on things above, not on earthly things like
Colossians 3:1-2 (NIV) says:

*"Since then, you have been raised with Christ, set your hearts
on things above, where Christ is, seated at the right hand of God.
Set your minds on things above, not on earthly things"*

Setting our minds on things above also implies that we
make heavenly things have the highest priority in our
hearts and minds; we treasure them above all else. That is
what the Bible says in Matthew 6:21 (NIV):

"For where your treasure is, there your heart will be also"

These scriptures imply that we are responsible for the
thoughts we think and encourages us to fill our minds
with things above, better things, beautiful things, and
positive things.
Once we occupy our minds with these, there will be no
room for negative, evil or sinful thoughts.

9. Forgive
A simple, beautiful; but dreaded word.

Forgiveness is a decision that originates from the mind. It is letting go of bitterness, resentment, anger, negative thoughts, thoughts of revenge for a wrong against us, etc.

God made it to be beautiful; a power and blessing release mechanism, but the enemy has perverted the thinking around it; making people believe that if they forgive, they are in some ways justifying the wrongdoings of others.

And so, they hold on to un-forgiveness and like someone that is holding unto a milestone in the sea, they are dragged down to the lowest parts; away from help and stuck in the depths, as un-forgiveness slowly eats them away like a cancer - shrouding them with fear, depression, frustration, anxiety, and loneliness; causing their spirits to be continuously sad and dejected.

I have never seen someone harbouring un-forgiveness that is truly happy and 100% healthy!

Proverbs 17:22b (NLT) says:
"but a broken spirit saps a person's strength."

They also prevent themselves from receiving forgiveness because the Bible says if you do not forgive others their sins your Father will not forgive your sins. (Matt.6:12, 15)

Sherry M. Jones writes:

"Forgiveness doesn't justify wrongdoings, but it releases your offenders, so they no longer control your emotions."

10. Look out for the way of escape

God makes an open road, but then man himself must walk in it. God controls circumstances, but man uses them. Now, before you begin to think looking out for a way of escape is cowardice, think again! In the place of "reason", truth can be skewed (Gen. 3:1); lies abound; and you are dealing with the father of all lies! (John 8:44). How do you suppose you can defeat him there? So, flee!

"Flee" is not a bad word.

- 1 Corinthians 6:18a says: *"Flee immorality."*
- 2 Timothy 2:22a says: *"Now flee from youthful lusts"*
- 1 Corinthians 10:14 says: *". . . flee from idolatry"*

There is a constant barrage; an unending assault from the enemy to take control of the battle ground of our minds! So, when we are beginning to feel overwhelmed and wanting to give in; read 1 Corinthians 10:13 where the Bible encourages us:

*"There hath no temptation taken you but such as is common to man: but God is faithful, who will not suffer you to be tempted above that ye are able; **but will with the temptation also make a way to escape, that ye may be able to bear it.**"*
Emphasis mine

So, what is this way of escape?
The way of escape depends on the type of attack! It could be anyone or all of the following we have considered:

- Deciding to shut evil thoughts out: not letting them in! Or interrupting them when they come! (Ephesians 4:27)
- Engaging in the daily renewal of your mind. (Romans 12:2)
- Aligning your thoughts with God's Words. (Colossians 3:1, Psalms 119:11)
- Preventing garbage from getting into your mind. (Galatians 6:7-8)
- Acknowledging the Lord; submitting to and revering Him. (Proverbs 3:6b)
- Spending time meditating on the Word of God. (Joshua 1:8)
- Living a life with a clear conscience (1 Timothy 1:19)
- Setting your minds on things above (Matthew 6:21)
- Living a life without offence - forgiveness (Matt.6:12, 15)

Before concluding this chapter, I will like to draw our attention to some things I have learnt.

- It is common knowledge that the mind is a battleground.

- Everyday our minds go through several thought interruptions; some are self-invoked; many others are not!
- It will help to be able to invoke thought interruptions yourself when needed.
- In the battle of the mind, never engage the enemy in his comfort zone – *the zone of reason!* If he drags you in there, flee into your comfort zone – *the zone of faith!*
- You do not get any brownie points for hanging around sin! Therefore, when God makes a way of escape for you, you are better off taking it! Flee!

"Flee" is not a bad word!

15
Seven Benefits

I T IS HUMAN NATURE TO BE naturally inclined towards accepting options when we realise there are inherent benefits in choosing them. What I refer to as the *"what's in it for me?"* mentality.

Of course, we can derive very many benefits from guarded hearts and minds.

So as not to disappoint you, I thought I should list out and consider only seven out of the many benefits that could be of guarded hearts and minds.

1. Your Life Will Be Changed for the Better

The very first benefit we shall look at is having a life changed for the better. If you are interested in truly changing your life, you must be ready to change the way you think!

With your thoughts aligned with the Word of God, change is inevitable! In fact, God Himself will do the transformation. Romans 12:2 (NLT) says:

*"Don't copy the behaviour and customs of this world, **but let God transform you into a new person by changing the way you think**. Then you will learn to know God's will for you, which is good and pleasing and perfect." Emphasis mine*

There are several ways of thinking that are beneficial to our health, progress, wealth, achievement, etc. Conversely, there are also ways of thinking that we have found to be detrimental. An old African proverb says:

Chapter Fifteen: Seven Benefits

"When there is no enemy within, the enemies outside cannot hurt you."

These *enemies within* are mostly thoughts in our heads that manifest as fear, doubt (either of God or self-doubt) anger, malice jealousy, etc. The truth is this: many know of these "enemies" but refuse to let them go! And they hang firmly to these "pets" of theirs while they slowly and silently eat them away like a "cancer" and quite often, literarily!

If the Almighty God can have good thoughts towards us, why then should we contradict Him and have negative thoughts about ourselves?
He said in Jeremiah 29:11(NKJV)

*"For I know the thoughts that I think toward you, says the Lord, thoughts of peace and **not of evil**, to give you a future and a hope." Emphasis mine.*

The things our minds are focused on; are the things we tend to attract to our lives. So, engage expectation positively. Proverbs 23:18 (KJV) says:

"For surely there is an end; and thine expectation shall not be cut off."

Expectation is a strong belief that something will happen or be the case. The Lord offers this huge advantage to His children who are right before Him. But why then do we waste this advantage and instead of expecting positivity, we settle for negativity?

When God wanted to use Gideon, He had to change the way he thought! Gideon saw himself as a *"nobody"*; he said in Judges 6:15b:
*"my family is poor in Manasseh, **and I am the least in my father's house**. (KJV)" Emphasis mine*

He had a limitation mentality; he could not see himself beyond the circumstances around him. His family, his community and his social status. But God saw him as a man of valour!
And so, in verse 16,
"The Lord answered him, "I will certainly be with you, and you will strike down the Midianites as [if they were only] one man." (AMP)

He needed to hear such words so that he could see himself as a man of valour! And so must we!

With our minds renewed, and our thinking ***recalibrated,*** we will, like Gideon, have our lives changed and begin to think beyond our self and circumstances-imposed boundaries and God Himself will transform our lives!

2. You Become a Candidate for the supernatural

The second benefit to be gained from a guarded heart and mind is that you very easily became a candidate for the supernatural, and *"impossible becomes nothing"*! Mark 9:23 (KJV) says:

*"Jesus said unto him, if thou canst believe, **all things are possible to him that believeth**" Emphasis mine*

Mark 11:23 (KJV) also says:

*"For verily I say unto you, that whosoever shall say unto this mountain, be thou removed, and be thou cast into the sea; **and shall not doubt in his heart, but shall believe that those things which he saith shall come to pass; he shall have whatsoever he saith.**" Emphasis mine*

3. You Will See God!

The Lord will reveal Himself and His goodness to you. Matt. 5:8 (AMP) says:

"Blessed [anticipating God's presence, spiritually mature] are the pure in heart [those with integrity, moral courage, and godly character], for they will see God"

In other words, blessed are those whose minds, motives, and principles are pure; who are genuine and decent, for they will see God!

Here on Earth

Enjoying communion with Him, both in private and public; beholding His beauty, His power and His glory. Psalm 27:4 (NIV) says:

*"One thing I ask from the Lord, this only do I seek: that I may dwell in the house of the Lord all the days of my life, **to gaze on the beauty of the Lord** and to seek him in his temple."* *Emphasis mine*

And in The World to Come

Where we shall see God in Christ 1 John 3:2 (NIV) says:

*"Dear friends, now we are children of God, and what we will be has not yet been made known. But we know that when Christ appears, we shall be like him, **for we shall see him as he is**" Emphasis mine*

4. You Will Receive a Blessing from The Lord

We all desire this one. A blessing from the Lord! Everyone desires God's blessings; to be fortunate, prosperous, and favoured by Him!
Psalm 24:3-4 (KJV) says:

*"Who shall ascend into the hill of the LORD? Or who shall stand in his holy place? **He that hath** clean hands, and **a pure heart**; who hath not lifted up his soul unto vanity, nor sworn*

*deceitfully. He **shall receive the blessing from the LORD**, and righteousness from the God of his salvation"* Emphasis mine.

5. You Will Have a Right Relationship with God.

With our thoughts properly channelled, we will have a right relationship with God, as He will give us His righteousness. Psalm 24:3-4 (KJV) says:

*"Who shall ascend into the hill of the LORD? Or who shall stand in his holy place? **He that hath** clean hands, and **a pure heart**; who hath not lifted up his soul unto vanity, nor sworn deceitfully. He **shall receive** the blessing from the LORD, and **righteousness from the God of his salvation**"* Emphasis mine.

There is no better feeling to have than the refreshing feeling of having unbroken fellowship with the Father; when your way pleases Him (Proverbs 16:7), and when your heart delights in Him (Psalm 37:4)

6. You will Experience Perfect and Constant Peace!

In a world plagued with all manner of chaos, the Lord will be your peace in the middle of it all if you guard your heart and mind!
Isaiah 26:3 (AMP) says:

"You will keep in perfect and constant peace the one whose **mind** *is steadfast [that is, committed and focused on You — in* **both inclination and character**], Because he trusts and takes refuge in You [with hope and confident expectation]."*

7. You will live a Healthy Life!

God wants us to be healthy - physically, emotionally and spiritually. We see this desire in 3 John 2 (AMP)

"Beloved, I pray that in every way you may succeed and prosper and be in good health [physically], just as [I know] your soul prospers [spiritually]."

A heart and mind that is guarded results in a life free of anxiety and consequently a healthy life! Proverbs 17:22a (MSG) says

"A cheerful disposition is good for your health; "

16

Final Words

OUR HEARTS AND MINDS ARE priceless possessions the Lord has blessed us with. They are worth giving everything we have to protect. They are very important to us because the things our hearts and minds are focused on, whether positive or negative are the things we tend to attract to our lives.

Unfortunately, the thoughts that constantly run through the minds of many people today are mostly negative due to the things happening around in the world! Thoughts hinged on fear, greed, deceit, etc. and they spend their conscious moments meditating on evil and perverted thoughts.

Genesis 6:5(KJV) says:
*"And God saw that the wickedness of man was great in the earth, and that every **imagination of the thoughts of his heart (mind)** was only evil continually." Emphasis mine*

What is your mind alive to?
Is it alive to, and conscious about, the things of the Spirit or the things of the flesh?
Is it aligned with thoughts that are *true, good,* and *right?* Or *false, bad* and *wrong?*
Is it continually good or continually evil?
Are you carefully and diligently guarding your heart and mind, or do you allow your mind to operate the "free range system"?

Chapter Sixteen: Final Words

If we fail to check our thought life, it can very quickly become our own worst enemy, poisoning us from within!

Sadly, most of the thinking over the years and up to today in the world has been carnal, ungodly, and uncontrolled. That is why our societies have turned out the way they are!

Romans 8:5-6 (NLT) says

"Those who are dominated by the sinful nature think about sinful things, but those who are controlled by the Holy Spirit think about things that please the Spirit. So letting your sinful nature control your mind leads to death. But letting the Spirit control your mind leads to life and peace."

This verse of scripture is akin to the chicken and egg situation; a sad unending cycle, and the very reason why we should diligently guard our hearts and minds!

I recently came across a quote:

"Be careful of your thoughts, for your thoughts become your words. Be careful of your words, for your words become your actions. Be careful of your actions, for your actions become your habits. Be careful of your habits, for your habits become your character. Be careful of your character, for your character becomes your destiny." – Author Unknown

This quote, without a doubt takes "some" of its roots from the Bible, (see Luke 6:45, Proverbs 18:21 and Heb. 5:14). The Bible in Proverbs 23:7 summarizes this quote with an amazing truth about our thoughts that so many people take for granted.

"For as he thinks in his heart, so is he." (NKJV)

The "control room" of life's outcomes is the heart and mind! That is why you become the way you think!

So, if your heart harbours evil, your mind will gravitate towards sinful thoughts and ultimately, you become sinful in nature and if you are dominated by the sinful nature you can only think about sinful things!
This principle of becoming what you think is clearly visible in our world today. You can easily tell the difference between the people who apply Philippians 4:8 from those who do not.
The fruits are obvious! Jesus said in Matt. 7:20 (NLT)

"Yes, just as you can identify a tree by its fruit, so you can identify people by their actions."

Those who practice Philippians 4:8 have sound minds and are mostly happier, optimistic, and fulfilled with their lives because their thoughts are filled with the more positive things in life.

Chapter Sixteen: Final Words

The reverse is the case for those who are not practicing Philippians 4:8; their thinking is mostly negative and perverted, and they are mostly unhappy, unfulfilled, pessimistic and depressed all the time!

They also have negative attitudes towards others and want them to be as unhappy as they are! As we have seen, the difference between these two types of people is in their thought life.

The Bible is very clearly telling us in Philippians 4:8 that we can all choose what to think about and dwell on.
The choice is ours to make; either align your thoughts to that which is true, good and right; and then become able to dwell on things that are excellent and worthy of praise. Or on the other hand, align your thoughts to that which is false, bad and wrong and become slaves to negative and pessimistic thoughts and consequently experience the fruits of such thoughts.
In Romans 12:3 (NIV) Paul writes:

"For by the grace given me I say to every one of you: **Do not think of yourself more highly than you ought**, *but rather think of yourself with sober judgment, in accordance with the faith God has distributed to each of you." Emphasis mine*

We are admonished to channel our thoughts appropriately; not to think of ourselves "more highly than we ought to".

If we allow God to change the way we think we will be able to learn (from Him) that which is good, pleasing and perfect! We can easily achieve this if we have our hearts and minds on constant guard.
Shalom!

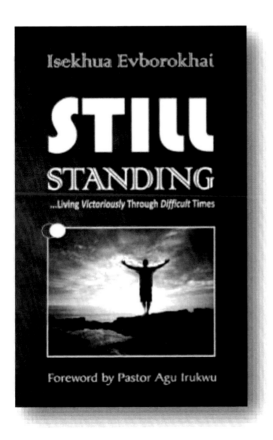

STILL STANDING
Living Victoriously Through Difficult Times
(Paperback)
See more about the book at:
http://isekhua.wordpress.com/
Copies available online on
http://lacepoint.ie/isekhua_evborokhai and your
local bookstore

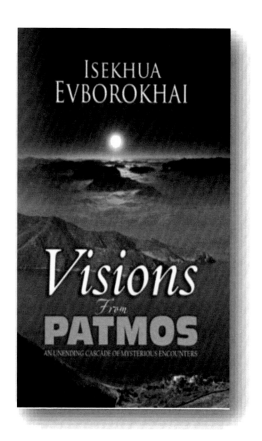

Visions from Patmos
An Unending Cascade of Mysterious Encounters
(Paperback)
See more about the book at:
http://isekhua.wordpress.com/
Copies available online on
http://lacepoint.ie/isekhua_evborokhai and your
local bookstore

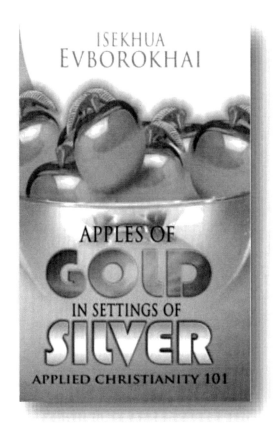

Apples of Gold in Settings of Silver
Applied Christianity 101 (Paperback)
See more about the book at:
http://isekhua.wordpress.com/
Copies available online on
http://lacepoint.ie/isekhua_evborokhai and your
local bookstore

Also by This Author

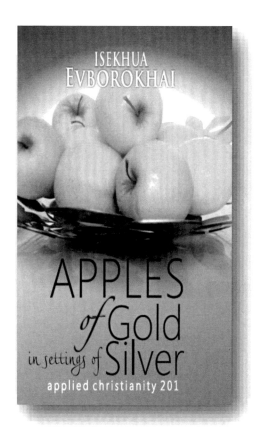

Apples of Gold in Settings of Silver *(Applied
Christianity 201)* (Paperback)
See more about the book at:
http://isekhua.wordpress.com/
Copies available online on
http://lacepoint.ie/isekhua_evborokhai and your
local bookstore

Apples of Gold in Settings of Silver *(Applied Christianity 301)* (Paperback)
See more about the book at:
http://isekhua.wordpress.com/
Copies available online on
http://lacepoint.ie/isekhua_evborokhai and your
local bookstore

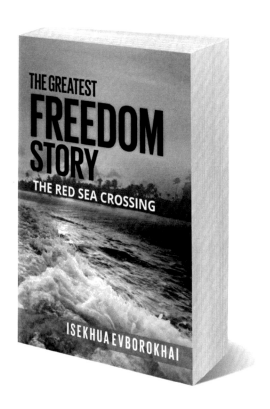

The Greatest Freedom Story *(The Red Sea Crossing)*
(eBook)
See more about the book at:
http://isekhua.wordpress.com/
FREE Copies available online on
http://lacepoint.ie/isekhua_evborokhai

The Relevant Life *(Ten Foundational Principles)*
(Paperback)
See more about the book at:
http://isekhua.wordpress.com/
Copies available online on
http://lacepoint.ie/isekhua_evborokhai and your
local bookstore

Also by This Author

ALL ABOUT YOU (CD)

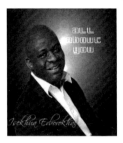 *"All About You"* inspired by the revelation of God's words was released in April 2011. This project comprising of over one hour of inspiring, upbeat, heartfelt, enthusiastic and energy-filled music is not only musically diverse but offers a richness and an atmosphere that will set your feet dancing and hearts worshipping!

http://isekhua.wordpress.com/all-about-you

Purchase a copy or download your copy from iTunes

https://itunes.apple.com/us/album/all-about-you/507880550

Purchase a copy or download your copy from cdbaby:

http://www.cdbaby.com/cd/isekhuaevborokhai

Also by This Author

THE ALMIGHTY REIGNS (CD)

"The Almighty Reigns" is a 10 track CD with nearly one hour of inspirational worship and upbeat songs across several genres; featuring Hezekiah Ezo and Mary "Mimi" Ogunniyi.!

https://isekhua.wordpress.com/the-almighty-reigns-the-cd/

Purchase a copy from Lacepoint Publishing:
https://lacepoint.ie/isekhua_evborokhai

Purchase a copy or download your copy from iTunes
https://itunes.apple.com/us/album/the-almighty-reigns/id1297862135

Purchase a copy or download your copy from cdbaby:
https://store.cdbaby.com/cd/isekhuaevborokhai2

CONTACT
Email
remisek@yahoo.com

Follow me on twitter:
@remsek

Subscribe to my blog at:

http://isekhua.wordpress.com/

Write to:

Isekhua Evborokhai
14, Rockfield Court
Hoey's Lane
Dundalk
Co Louth
Republic of Ireland